A CHORUS OF DISAPPROVAL

A CHORUS
OF DISAPPROVAL

ALAN AYCKBOURN

faber and faber
LONDON · BOSTON

First published in 1986
by Faber and Faber Limited
3 Queen Square London WC1N 3AU

Filmset by Wilmaset Birkenhead Wirral
Printed in Great Britain by
Whitstable Litho Limited
Whitstable Kent
All rights reserved

British Library Cataloguing in Publication Data

Ayckbourn, Alan
A chorus of disapproval
I. Title
822′.914   PR6051.735
ISBN 0–571–13917–5

A Chorus of Disapproval was first presented at the Stephen Joseph Theatre, Scarborough, on 2 May 1984 with the following cast:

GUY JONES	Lennox Greaves
DAFYDD AP LLEWELLYN	Russell Dixon
HANNAH LLEWELLYN	Alwyne Taylor
BRIDGET BAINES	Jane Hollowood
MR AMES	Paul Todd
ENID WASHBROOK	Dorcas Jones
REBECCA HUNTLEY-PIKE	Heather Stoney
FAY HUBBARD	Lesley Meade
IAN HUBBARD	Mark Jax
JARVIS HUNTLEY-PIKE	Alan Thompson
TED WASHBROOK	Robert Cotton
CRISPIN USHER	Daniel Flynn
LINDA WASHBROOK	Caroline Webster

and subsequently at the Olivier Theatre, London, on 1 August 1985 with the following cast:

GUY JONES	Bob Peck
DAFYDD AP LLEWELLYN	Michael Gambon
HANNAH LLEWELLYN	Imelda Staunton
BRIDGET BAINES	Jenny Galloway
MR AMES	Paul Todd
ENID WASHBROOK	Jane Wenham
REBECCA HUNTLEY-PIKE	Moira Redmond
FAY HUBBARD	Gemma Craven
IAN HUBBARD	Paul Bentall
JARVIS HUNTLEY-PIKE	David Ryall
TED WASHBROOK	James Hayes
CRISPIN USHER	Daniel Flynn
LINDA WASHBROOK	Kelly Hunter

Director	Alan Ayckbourn
Settings	Alan Tagg
Musical Director	Paul Todd

Characters

GUY JONES

DAFYDD AP LLEWELLYN
HANNAH LLEWELLYN

IAN HUBBARD
FAY HUBBARD

JARVIS HUNTLEY-PIKE
REBECCA HUNTLEY-PIKE

TED WASHBROOK
ENID WASHBROOK
LINDA WASHBROOK, *their daughter*

BRIDGET BAINES

CRISPIN USHER

MR AMES
RAYMOND
Stage Managers (non-speaking)

The action occurs between the first rehearsal and first performance of an amateur production of Gay's *The Beggar's Opera*
(February–May). It takes place in and around a small provincial
theatre.

ACT ONE

The lights come up abruptly on a stage filled with people and we are
suddenly and unexpectedly into the final moments of a first
performance of an amateur production of Gay's The Beggar's
Opera. *The performance by PALOS (The Pendon Amateur Light*
Operatic Society) is filled with gusto and enthusiasm. What it lacks
in polish (in some quarters) it makes up for in flourish. Among the
performers are centre, on a small raised platform, GUY JONES
(Macheath).
He is surrounded by his 'doxies'. Amongst these are HANNAH
LLEWELLYN *(Polly Peachum),* LINDA WASHBROOK *(Lucy*
Lockit), REBECCA HUNTLEY-PIKE *(Mrs Vixen),* FAY HUBBARD
(Dolly Trull), BRIDGET BAINES *(Jenny Diver) and others. Also*
present are TED *and* ENID WASHBROOK *(Mr and Mrs Peachum),*
IAN HUBBARD *(Matt of the Mint),* CRISPIN USHER *(Filch),*
JARVIS HUNTLEY-PIKE *(Lockit) and others. At the piano,*
MR AMES *(The Beggar).*

GUY: *(As Macheath)*
 Thus I stand like the Turk, with his Doxies around;
 From all sides their Glances his Passion confound;
 For black, brown and fair, his Inconstancy burns,
 And the different Beauties subdue him by turns:
 Each calls forth her Charms to provoke his Desires:
 Though willing to all; with but one he retires.
 But think of this Maxim, and put off your Sorrow,
 The Wretch of To-day, may be happy To-morrow.
ALL: Each calls forth her Charms and provokes his Desires:
 Though willing to all; with but one he retires.
 But think of this Maxim, and put off your Sorrow,
 The Wretch of To-day, may be happy To-morrow *(etc.)*
 (The dance that accompanies the final chorus finally finishes
 with a triumphant tableau. The lights dim slightly to indicate
 the curtain has fallen. The company shuffles quickly into fresh
 positions. Muffled applause is heard. The lights brighten as the

*curtain goes up and the applause becomes louder and clearer. The
company is all smiles at once. Several of these pre-rehearsed
variants follow with finally* GUY *as Macheath taking a solo call
and being applauded by his fellow artistes. Graciously, he presents
his two leading ladies,* HANNAH *(Polly) and* LINDA *(Lucy).
Both, in turn, are presented with bouquets. Next, the company
turns in the direction of* MR AMES *(The Beggar) at the piano who
rises and makes a sheepish acknowledgement. The general bow
follows and, at this point, with a sort of reluctant alacrity, the
producer,* DAFYDD LLEWELLYN, *springs on to the stage from the
auditorium. The cast, in turn, applauds him. Looking somewhat
incongruous in his modern clothes, he bows modestly and finally
raises his hands for silence. The applause ceases.)*

DAFYDD: Ladies and gentlemen, thank you all for that
wonderful, wonderful reception. There are a million people
I ought to thank. There are a million people I'd like to
thank and there are a million people I'm afraid I'm not
going to thank, at least by name or you'll be sitting here till
tomorrow morning.
(He laughs. The cast smiles with relief.)
I will, if I may, restrict myself to saying this. Thank you,
wonderful cast. Thank you, wonderful, wonderful Stage
Management. Thank you, marvellous audience. But thank
you most of all to one individual without whom none of this
could have happened. He joined PALOS but a few weeks
ago. The emergency occurred and the man rose to the
occasion. What more can I say? – He's been . . . Well, your
reception said it all. Ladies and gentlemen, our very special
Macheath, Mr Guy Jones.
*(DAFYDD turns and presents GUY who acknowledges fresh
applause. Again, the cast joins in. The curtain falls finally. The
lights again dim to indicate this and the applause becomes
muffled, finally dying out. The cast starts to disperse, chattering
and laughing and moving towards the dressing room. GUY,
quite suddenly, is all alone. No one, once the curtain has fallen,
speaks to or even acknowledges him. He stands for a moment
before starting to remove his costume, beginning with his wig
and hat, then jacket and cravat. Stage managers begin to move*

round him re-setting and striking props, including the raised
platform. In time, the remaining stage lights go out and are
replaced by harsh working lights. Similarly the stage reverts
from a performance to a rehearsal state. HANNAH, still in her
basic Polly costume, comes on carrying GUY's clothes. She
watches him for a second.)

HANNAH: (*Softly*) Well done.

GUY: Mmm?

HANNAH: Well done.

GUY: (*Dully*) Thank you.

HANNAH: (*Indicating his clothes*) Here are your . . .
(GUY *makes no move.*)
I'll leave them here . . .
(HANNAH *puts the clothes gently on a table and makes to
leave.*)

GUY: Thanks.

HANNAH: (*Turning as she goes*) I – (*Changing her mind*) Right.
I must . . . Goodbye.

GUY: Yes. Goodbye.
(HANNAH *goes.* GUY *finishes changing, finally putting on his
mac. He seems about to leave but turns in the doorway and
surveys the darkened stage. We hear the distant sound of the
piano playing 'Youth's the Season made for Joys'. It's a
fragment, a wistful echo of his memory. It is now three to four
months earlier. February and very cold. Voices and laughter are
heard from a distance in the dressing rooms offstage.* GUY,
*having entered from the street, stands uncertainly wondering
whether to proceed further.* BRIDGET, *in coat, hat and boots,
enters with a small rehearsal table which she bangs down rather
noisily. At first appearance she is a rather graceless, galumphing
girl who has long ago dispensed with social niceties and
conventional sexual role-playing. She gives no sign of having
seen* GUY *but continues on her way.* GUY *makes a little gurgling
sound in his throat.*)

BRIDGET: (*Turning back at the last minute*) Did you want
somebody?

GUY: Mr Jones.

BRIDGET: Mr Jones?

GUY: Yes.

BRIDGET: No.

GUY: No?

BRIDGET: No. No Mr Jones here.

GUY: No, no . . .

BRIDGET: This is the Operatic Society.

GUY: Yes, yes.

BRIDGET: We haven't any Mr Jones.

GUY: No. You won't have.

BRIDGET: No?

GUY: Well, you might have but . . . No, I'm Mr Jones.

BRIDGET: You're Mr Jones?

GUY: Yes. (*Slight pause*.) Sorry.

BRIDGET: We'll start again, shall we?

GUY: Yes.

BRIDGET: I've just come in. Right?

GUY: Right.

BRIDGET: OK. So. Who do you want?

GUY: Mr Llewellyn. Mr – (*looking at an envelope he has taken from his pocket*) – Mr D. Ap Llewellyn.

BRIDGET: Is he expecting you?

GUY: Yes, I think so. He said round about this time.

BRIDGET: Wait there, then. Mr Jones, yes?

GUY: Yes.

(BRIDGET *goes*.

GUY *hops around a little. Half because of nerves, half because of the cold. He spies a piano in the corner and moves to it. From the envelope he is holding he produces a small piece of music, obviously torn from a book. With an inexperienced finger, he taps out the odd note and attempts to match them with his voice. Whatever he plays appears to be outside his range. He clears his throat but it's quite obvious that his voice has packed up completely. With sudden determination,* GUY *screws up the piece of music, stuffs it into his pocket and marches towards the door. Before he can leave, there is a burst of chatter from off and* DAFYDD *enters. He is a busy, slightly overweight, energetic man in his late thirties. A live-wire. The mainspring of the society. Never using one word where three*

12

will do, never walking when he can hurry. Whatever the temperature, DAFYDD *always appears to find it a little on the warm side.*)

DAFYDD: (*Seeing* GUY) My dear chap, I'm so sorry. I'm deeply sorry. I knew you were coming. I wrote down you were coming. It slipped my mind. How do you do? Dafydd ap Llewellyn. Good of you to come along. We're on our first stages of rehearsal. Just getting started. Broken for tea for ten minutes.

GUY: Ah. Yes.

DAFYDD: (*Calling*) Mr Ames? I'll just fetch Mr Ames in and he can play for you. Brought something along to sing, have you?

GUY: Well, I had sort of –

DAFYDD: (*Calling*) Mr Ames? Otherwise we've got plenty of bits and pieces lying around, you know. And of course, Mr Ames, he's encyclopaedic. He's played practically every musical comedy you could name. Choose a key, choose a tune, choose a tempo, he's away – where the bloody hell is he? Excuse me. (*He moves to the door, calling*) Mr Ames? – ah, there you are. This is Mr Ames.

(MR AMES *enters. He is a small, intensely shy man whose silent, unobtrusive personality is in direct contrast to that of* DAFYDD.)

DAFYDD: Mr Ames, this is Mr – God, I'm afraid I don't even know your name – Mr . . . ?

GUY: Jones.

DAFYDD: Mr Jones – not Welsh, are you?

GUY: No. No. 'Fraid not. From Leeds.

DAFYDD: (*Dubiously*) Leeds?

GUY: Originally.

DAFYDD: Originally from Leeds. Right. This is our Mr Ames. Mr Ames, Mr Jones is going to sing for us. Give us an idea of his range. And intonation. Which is a polite way of saying can he sing in tune? (*He laughs.*) If not, welcome to the club. What are you, tenor, are you?

GUY: I think I'm a sort of light baritone. I think.

DAFYDD: Oh yes? Light baritone, eh? Yes, we've got plenty of those lurking in the back row, haven't we, Mr Ames? They're what we call our down the octave brigade.

GUY: (*Laughing*) Yes, yes . . .

DAFYDD: Come on then. Let's have a listen. Did you say you had some music? Or shall we ask Mr Ames to rifle through his golden treasure chest of memories?

GUY: (*Fumbling for his music*) No, I've brought . . . (*Unable to find it and rummaging through his pockets*) Just a second . . .

DAFYDD: Bit of *Merry Widow*? Fancy that?

GUY: (*Somewhat panic-stricken at the thought*) No, no, please . . .

DAFYDD: *West Side Story*? *Oklahoma*? *The King and I*? (MR AMES *plays a bar of this last.*)

GUY: (*Finding his music at last*) No. Here we are. Found it. Here. (*He holds up the crumpled piece of music.*)

DAFYDD: Is that it?

GUY: Sorry.

DAFYDD: You shouldn't have splashed out like that, you know. Not just for an audition. (*He laughs again, and takes the scrap of music from* GUY *and gives it to* MR AMES.) Here we are, Mr Ames. Second Act of *Tannhäuser*, by the look of it. (*He laughs.*) No, I'm sorry, Mr Jones. We're only having a little joke. Don't mind us, you'll get used to it. Possibly. (*Briskly*) Right. Seriously for a moment. Be serious, Llewellyn, boy. What have we got here? (*Putting on his reading glasses*) My word, my word. You still claim you're not Welsh? What does that say there, Mr Ames? What does it say to you? 'All Through the Night'. '*Ar hyd y nos*'.

GUY: Yes. Coincidence.

DAFYDD: (*Mock serious*) Well. I don't know. Should we allow a man from Leeds to sing this, Mr Ames? Eh? What do you think?

GUY: It was just the only song I happen to . . .

DAFYDD: Well. Seeing your name is Jones. Maybe. Special dispensation, eh?

GUY: (*Gamely trying to keep up with the joke*) Thank you very much . . .

DAFYDD: Just this once.

GUY: It was the only song I knew in the piano stool. My mother used to sing it. Years ago.

DAFYDD: Your mother's Welsh, then?

GUY: No.

DAFYDD: But she sings?

GUY: No, she . . .

DAFYDD: Bring her down. Bring her down next time with you.

GUY: No, she's dead.

DAFYDD: (*Sadly*) Ah. Well. Too late then. Too late. Sad. Can you play that, do you think, Mr Ames?

MR AMES: Yes, yes . . . (*He plays a chord or two, peering at the music.*

ENID WASHBROOK appears in the doorway during this. Behind ENID, her daughter LINDA cranes round her to catch a glimpse of the newcomer.)

ENID: Are we starting again, Dafydd?

DAFYDD: In just one moment, Enid, just one moment. We'll give you a call. We're just going to hear this gentleman sing . . .

ENID: Oh, right. Excuse us, won't you . . .

DAFYDD: We'll give you a call.

ENID: (*To GUY, as they go*) Good luck.

GUY: Thank you.

(*ENID and LINDA go out.*)

DAFYDD: Now, Mr Jones, the million dollar question. Are you going to sing this in Welsh or in English?

GUY: Well, I'm sorry, in English if that's all right . . .

DAFYDD: (*Hopping about in mock pain*) Oh, oh, oh, oh . . . Like 'Pomp and Circumstance' in Japanese . . . If you must, if you must . . . Right. When you're ready, Mr Ames. Take it away . . .

(*MR AMES plays the introduction. DAFYDD moves away slightly. GUY opens his mouth to sing. Before he can do so, DAFYDD is there before him sounding off in a full Welsh tenor.*)

DAFYDD: *Holl amrantau'r ser ddywedant, Ar hyd y nos,*
Dyma'r ffordd i fro gogon-iant, Ar hyd y nos;
Go-lau a-rall yw tywyll-wch, I arddangos gwir brydferthwch,
Teulu'r nefoedd mewn ta-welwch, Ar hyd y nos.

(DAFYDD *stops singing*. MR AMES *stops playing. There is a respectful silence.*)
Sorry. I'm sorry. I sincerely beg your pardon, Mr Jones. Every time I hear . . . (*He breaks off, too moved to continue. Then, clapping* GUY *on the shoulder*) It's all yours. Take it away, boy.

GUY: (*Horrified*) Right.
(MR AMES *re-starts the introduction.* DAFYDD *moves away to the far reaches of the auditorium.* GUY, *by now very nervous, misses the introduction first time round but manages on the second.*)
(*Nervously*) While the moon her watch is keeping,
All through the night,
While the we–

DAFYDD: (*Calling from the darkness*) Mr Jones, sorry to interrupt you just as you were getting underway. That's lovely. Very pleasant. A little tip. Just try facing out this way a bit more, would you? You're not in need of the music, are you?

GUY: (*Straining to see* DAFYDD) No, no.

DAFYDD: No, it didn't appear you were reading it. (*Waving* GUY *away from the safety of the piano.*) Now. Just try placing your weight equally on both your feet. Legs slightly apart. That's it. A bit more. Now, can you feel yourself balanced, can you?

GUY: Yes, yes.

DAFYDD: Singing is a great deal to do with balance, Mr Jones. Balance, you see. You can't sing on one leg now, can you? You'd feel unbalanced.

GUY: Yes, yes.

DAFYDD: Good. Shoulders back, then. Shoulders right back, man.

GUY: Yes.

DAFYDD: That's better. That's better. Now, before you start this time, Mr Jones, I want you for a moment to breathe, if you would. Like this.
(DAFYDD *demonstrates noisily from the darkness.*)
In through the nose, you see, out through the mouth. That's it. And again. Deep as you can, that's it.

(GUY *sways and staggers.*)

No, no. There's no need to hyperventilate. Breathe normally, that's all. Now, Mr Jones, can you feel all that air, can you? In your passages? Can you feel it rushing along your passages?

GUY: Yes, yes.

DAFYDD: Blowing the cobwebs from your passages?

GUY: (*Coughing slightly*) Yes.

(*From this point, people begin to assemble, unseen by* GUY, *to listen to him. First to appear are* JARVIS HUNTLEY-PIKE *and* TED WASHBROOK. JARVIS *is a man in his late fifties – the epitome of a 'Knowing Northerner'.* TED, *ten years younger, is a mild, pleasant, abstracted, ineffectual man.*)

DAFYDD: Now you look like a real singer, Mr Jones. From the top, please, Mr Ames. From the top.

(MR AMES *starts again.*)

(*Over the introduction*) Let it flow out of you, Mr Jones. Let it flow. It's a song that sings itself, you see. Like a river. (*Singing*) *Holl amrantau'r* . . . You see?

GUY: Yes, yes. (*He waits for the introduction to come round again.*)

(FAY HUBBARD *and* ENID WASHBROOK *enter and stand watching.* FAY *is an extremely attractive woman in her thirties. One of the local younger married jet-set.* ENID, *a little older, is a careworn sort of woman, even less effectual than her husband,* TED.)

(*Singing*) While the moon her watch is keeping,
    All through the night,
While the weary world is sleeping,
    All through the night.

DAFYDD: (*Over this, as he sings*) Good, good. Don't hunch. Don't hunch. You can't sing if you're hunched, Mr Jones. Good. (*Joining in with him, singing*) All through the night.

(LINDA WASHBROOK *and* CRISPIN USHER *have meantime entered.* LINDA *is the nicely brought-up, rather petulant daughter of her over-anxious parents,* TED *and* ENID. CRISPIN, *her currently unsuitable boyfriend, is a tough, hostile young man very much at odds with his present environment and with most of the Society.*)

17

GUY: O'er my bosom gently stealing,
Visions of delight revealing,
Breathes a pure and holy feeling,
   All through the night.
(*As he reaches the final stages of the song,* IAN HUBBARD *and* REBECCA HUNTLEY-PIKE *appear. They are followed by* BRIDGET. IAN, FAY's *husband, is almost her male counterpart. An ambitious young man with a cultivated laid-back cool designed to make money and charm women, in that order.* REBECCA, JARVIS's *wife, is younger than he by a few years. She has that dignified appearance of one who has just had several stiff drinks. Maybe she has.* GUY *finishes.*)

DAFYDD: (*Applauding*) Bravo. Bravo.
(*The rest of the company join in his applause.* GUY *jumps in alarm, unaware that such a large audience has gathered.*)
Ah, here they all are. Ladies and gentlemen, may I present a new member of our Society. Mr Jones, who has just passed with flying colours.
(*A burst of general chatter and greeting.*)
(*Through this*) Now, these are – these are a lot of different people who are going to have to introduce themselves. I can't be doing with that.
(*The following section overlaps.*)

REBECCA: Hallo, welcome. Is he playing Matt the Mint?

DAFYDD: Ah, well. Maybe, maybe.

REBECCA: We need a Matt the Mint. He'd be wonderful. Lovely voice.

GUY: (*Smiling gratefully*) Thank you.

REBECCA: Isn't it? A lovely voice. Most unusual.

FAY: Yes.

REBECCA: Mr Jones, is it?

GUY: Guy.

REBECCA: Guy. Oh, that's a nice name. I like the name, Guy, don't you? It's very masculine.

ENID: Manly, yes. Manly.

FAY: Frightfully, yes.

IAN: Are we going on or going home? I'm for going home.

JARVIS: I don't care what we do. Five past ten, I'm in the pub. I tell you.

DAFYDD: Everybody, could I have your attention? Please. Just a second, everybody.

BRIDGET: (*Shouting*) Shut up!

REBECCA: I do wish she wouldn't shout like that.

DAFYDD: Now, everybody, I must apolo–

REBECCA: Why can't she just ask people to be quiet?

DAFYDD: I must apologize, ladies and gentlemen, for making much, much slower progress than I anticipated. So, apologies for calling you all in and for keeping you hanging around. Mind you, I must say this evening has not been wasted. We've done some good solid groundwork and that's surely going to pay off later. So what I'd like to do just before we call it a night, is a quick recap from the top. OK? All right, Ted?

TED: From the top?

DAFYDD: If you'd be so kind. OK, Mr Ames?

REBECCA: Oh, good. We can watch.

TED: (*To* MR AMES) We're going from the top, apparently.

MR AMES: Right.

JARVIS: What's the time, then?

IAN: We've got half an hour yet.

FAY: (*To* REBECCA) Do you want to go over now?

REBECCA: Not on your life. We've all been sitting back there in the cold for two and a half hours. Let's see what they've been up to, for heaven's sake.

DAFYDD: So. The house lights dim. Blackout. Mr Ames in position. Ted in position. And then the soft glow of lamp light very gently – and – cue.

MR AMES: (*Reading as The Beggar*) If Poverty be a Title to Poetry, I am sure Nobody can dispute mine. I own myself of the Company of Beggars; and I make one at their Weekly Festivals at St Giles. I have a small Yearly Salary for my Catches, and am welcome to Dinner there whenever I please, which is more than most Poets can say.

TED: (*Reading as Player*) As we believe by the Muses, 'tis but Gratitude in us to encourage Poetical Merit wherever we find it. Be the Author who he will, we push his Play as far as it will go. So (though you are in want) I wish you Success heartily. But I see 'tis time for us to withdraw; the Actors are preparing to begin. Play away the Overture.

(TED *exits with a flourish. Then reappears somewhat sheepishly having evidently gone off the wrong way. He tiptoes across to the correct exit, and, with an apologetic look at* DAFYDD, *goes. A silence.*)

DAFYDD: (*Choosing to ignore* TED's *mistake*) Splendid, splendid. Well done.

REBECCA: Is that it?

DAFYDD: Yes, yes. So far.

REBECCA: That's all you've done?

DAFYDD: Yes.

REBECCA: My God. We're not on till page 30. When do you want us? Next June?

DAFYDD: All right, all right.

TED: (*Anxiously*) Was that OK?

DAFYDD: Marvellous, Ted, marvellous.

REBECCA: Riveting. Can't wait to find out who done it. Right, let's have that drink, then.

(*A general move to the door. Chatter.*)

JARVIS: (*Confidentially to* DAFYDD) Just looking at that scene, I think you'll find it might benefit from a bit of gesture, you know . . .

DAFYDD: (*Gathering up his things*) Yes, yes, thank you, Jarvis. I'm sure it would . . .

JARVIS: It's just in those days they used their arms a lot, you know. Great deal of gesture.

DAFYDD: Yes, well, I'll be stuffing it full of gestures at a later stage, Jarvis. Be patient. You won't see the stage for arm movements . . .

JARVIS: You don't mind me saying . . . ?

DAFYDD: Not at all. It's just, you know with Ted you can't go too fast. It takes a month or two just to get him pointing the right way . . . You know old Ted. (*He laughs.*)

JARVIS: (*Going out*) You don't mind me coming up with the odd idea, do you, now and again?

DAFYDD: Not at all, Jarvis, any time . . . feel free . . .

(JARVIS *goes out*.)

(*Calling*) You really must do a production yourself some time. (*Muttering*) And I'll come and bugger yours up, you interfering old fascist . . . (*Seeing* GUY *is still there*) Ah, Mr Jones, you're still here. Splendid. Fancy a quick pint? We usually go across the road to The Fleece. He's a cantankerous old bastard, the chap who runs it, but it's the best pint for 30 miles . . .

GUY: Righto. Splendid. Lead on.

(BRIDGET *comes from backstage*.)

DAFYDD: Ah, Bridget. You'll switch off, will you?

BRIDGET: Yes.

DAFYDD: Bridget's our stage manager. Also playing Jenny Diver. We couldn't function at all without Bridget. She's the one who keeps us all sane, Mr Jones.

GUY: Good for you.

(*He smiles at* BRIDGET. BRIDGET *doesn't react*. DAFYDD *gathers together his papers*. GUY *perseveres cheerily*.)

I'm just going over the road to brave this cantankerous old publican. See you over there, perhaps?

DAFYDD: You certainly will. Bridget's his daughter.

GUY: Ah.

BRIDGET: Are we picking it up tomorrow from where we stopped?

DAFYDD: Yes, we'll carry straight on, my love.

BRIDGET: Right. From the bottom of page 1, then.

DAFYDD: Oh, now please, please. Don't you start, there's a dear. (*To* GUY) Fit then, are you, Mr Jones? Right. Away we go.

(*The scene changes to the pub. A crowded saloon bar containing most of the Society.* DAFYDD *and* GUY *jostle their way in*.)

DAFYDD: (*Shouting above the din*) Tends to get a bit crowded but it's worth it for the beer.

IAN: (*Calling across*) Pint, Daf?

DAFYDD: Oh, bless you, my love. Though I think it's my shout.

IAN: It's all right, I'm getting them.

DAFYDD: Pint for you, Mr Jones?

GUY: Would it be all right to have a gin and tonic?

DAFYDD: Gin and tonic? That's what they're drinking in Leeds, is it? Right. (*Calling*) Ian? Can you get this fellow a gin and tonic?

IAN: Gin and tonic. Is he coming in here a lot, is he?

DAFYDD: (*Laughing, to* GUY) You mustn't mind him. He's got a great sense of humour. Ian and his brother, they're in partnership together. The brother does the work. Ian spends the money. (*He laughs.*)

REBECCA: (*Her voice ringing across the pub, to* GUY) We've all voted for you to play Matt the Mint. We think you're lovely.

GUY: Thank you.

DAFYDD: Mrs Huntley-Pike. Another singer we put well to the back. In her case preferably in the car park.

GUY: Like me, you mean? (*He laughs.*)

DAFYDD: God, no. You haven't heard her. If she sang in the dairy she'd make cheese. I tell you. Married, of course, to old Councillor Huntley-Potty-Pike. One of the whizz kids on our Council. Which explains why this town's in the state it is.

IAN: (*Arriving with the drinks*) There you go.

DAFYDD: Ah, thank you, Ian. Bless you.

IAN: Gin and tonic.

GUY: Thank you very much.

IAN: Hope you don't want ice because he hasn't got any.

DAFYDD: He's got ice, the miserable old sod. He just hides it. You can't charge for it, don't put it out. That's his maxim. His beer mats are screwed to the bar. Cheers.

IAN: Cheers.

GUY: Here's to the – production.

DAFYDD: Yes, why not? Here's to it. *The Beggar's Opera.* (*Waving his glass in the direction of the women's table*) To *The Beggar's Opera.*

FAY: (*Echoing*) Yes. *The Beggar's Opera.*

REBECCA: Hear, hear. *The Beggar's Opera.*

GUY: When do we – when does it – start? Open?
(*A phone rings faintly from behind the bar.*)

DAFYDD: Oh, not till May. We've got three and a half months yet. Still, with dear old Ted there, I think we're going to need it. Mind you, we've got used to him now, haven't we, Ian? We had him one time in, what was it, *Sound of Music*, was it? –

(BRIDGET *has appeared the other side of the bar and is now calling and waving in an attempt to attract* DAFYDD'*s attention.*)

BRIDGET: (*Calling*) Dafydd. Dafydd.

IAN: (*Seeing her, to* DAFYDD) Dafydd, I think she wants you.

DAFYDD: (*Turning*) Hallo. Yes, my love?

BRIDGET: (*Miming*) Phone. Phone.

DAFYDD: Ah. Telephone. Do excuse me, won't you? (*To* GUY, *handing him his pint*) Hang on to that a second, would you mind?

GUY: (*Taking it*) Certainly.

DAFYDD: (*Moving away*) I trust you.

BRIDGET: It's Hannah for you.

DAFYDD: What the hell's she want . . .

(DAFYDD *goes to a corner of the bar, takes the receiver, sticks a finger in his ear and starts a conversation which we cannot hear. With the departure of* DAFYDD, *the small talk between* IAN *and* GUY *seems thin on the ground.*)

IAN: Cheers.

GUY: Cheers.

(*Pause.*

GUY, *rather nervously, takes a swig of beer.*)

IAN: Get on well with Dafydd, do you?

GUY: Well, yes, I think –

IAN: I hope so, because you're drinking his beer.

GUY: Oh, God, yes. Sorry. Do you know that's something that I'm always . . . well, not always – but occasionally –

(FAY *approaches them and interrupts.*)

FAY: Darling, have you got a light? They're all dreary non-smokers over there. (*Smiling at* GUY, *her reason for joining them*) Hallo, I'm Fay. I'm this thing's wife. How do you do.

GUY: Hallo.

FAY: You don't know what a pleasure it is to see a new man in the Society. It's mostly filled with us boring women. Dreadful.

GUY: (*Gallantly*) Dreadful for some, perhaps.

FAY: (*Throwing her head back with a tinkling laugh*) Yes. Depends on your point of view.

IAN: (*Not quite to himself*) Jesus . . .

(*He moves away to put his glass on the bar.*)

FAY: (*After him*) Where are you off to?

IAN: Going to bring the car round. Why?

FAY: Heavens and not yet closing time. What's come over him? (*She smiles at* GUY *again.*) Hallo.

GUY: (*A fraction uneasily*) Hallo. Well, I suppose I must be making a move, too.

FAY: You got a car? Only otherwise we could drop you.

GUY: No, thanks. I'm mobile . . .

JARVIS: (*Who is heading towards them with some empty glasses*) I say, I say.

FAY: (*Under her breath*) Oh, no. Quick, hide, take cover.

JARVIS: (*Reaching them*) I say. Yes. You. You're a Scotchman, aren't you?

GUY: No, no.

JARVIS: They're the only people who do that, you know. The Scotties. That's the way you tell 'em.

FAY: Tell what?

JARVIS: Look, look, look. Look, you see. Glass in each hand. Whisky, beer. Whisky, beer. That's the way they do it. Scotty, right?

GUY: No.

JARVIS: Always tell 'em. Always tell 'em. (*He moves away.*)

GUY: I didn't understand that at all.

FAY: (*Laughing*) Don't worry. He's completely mad.

GUY: Ah.

FAY: Quite harmless, though.

GUY: Glad to hear it.

FAY: No, it's her you've got to watch. (*She nods towards* REBECCA.) Hallo. (*She smiles again at* GUY.)

(IAN *returns from the bar en route to the door. He drags* FAY *out with him.*)

(*As she's whisked away*) I think this means we're going. Goodnight, then.

GUY: Goodnight.

IAN: 'Night.

FAY: Do excuse us. Some nights he can hardly contain himself.
(FAY *and* IAN *go out.*)

JARVIS: (*From the bar calling to* GUY) Hey! I say, you, Jimmy
. . . Jimmy.

GUY: (*Mystified*) Me?

JARVIS: You want another wee dram in there . . . ?

GUY: No thank you, this is gin . . .

JARVIS: (*To* BRIDGET) And a wee one for our friend from over
the border.

GUY: Oh, Lord . . .
(*Over in the other corner of the bar,* MR AMES *begins playing
the piano. Shortly,* TED *starts singing and is then joined by most
of the others.*)

TED: (*Singing*) Fill ev'ry Glass, for Wine inspires us,
      And fires us
With Courage, Love and Joy.

ALL: Fill ev'ry Glass, for Wine inspires us,
      And fires us
With Courage, Love and Joy.

TED: Women and Wine should Life employ.
Is there ought else on earth desirous?
Fill ev'ry Glass, for Wine inspires us,
      And fires us
With Courage, Love and Joy.

ALL: Women and Wine should Life employ (*etc.*)
(GUY *stands bemusedly as this starts. His bemusement slightly
increases as* JARVIS *passes him and pours a large scotch into
his gin glass.* JARVIS *moves to the piano and joins the
singers.* DAFYDD, *having finished on the phone, rejoins*
GUY.)

DAFYDD: (*Over the singing*) Good old Ted. Get him near a piano,
he's away. Marvellous music, isn't it? All traditional tunes,
you know. All the tunes Gay used were traditional.

GUY: Really?

DAFYDD: Still as fresh as they ever were . . .
(BRIDGET, *from the other side of the bar, appears, ringing a*

large bell. The singing stops.)

BRIDGET: My dad says he's not licensed for music and dancing and would you please stop that bloody row . . .
(*A chorus of booing and catcalls.*)
Only he didn't say please, like I did.

CRISPIN: Why's he got a piano for, then?

BRIDGET: That's reserved for private functions . . .

REBECCA: This is a private function . . .

CRISPIN: Yes. Bugger off . . .

BRIDGET: Hey, you. Watch your language, you. You're not in the gutter now, you know . . .

JARVIS: (*To* MR AMES) Play a Highland Fling for the Scotty over there . . .

BRIDGET: Sorry. Those are the rules of the house. Thank you very much. And last orders, please . . .

CRISPIN: You want to get rid of that piano if people can't use it . . .

BRIDGET: (*Ignoring this*) Last orders, please.

LINDA: It's a filthy place, anyhow.

BRIDGET: You know where to go if you don't like it, don't you? Sitting there drinking half of shandy for three hours. We can do without you for a kick off . . .

LINDA: What's it got to do with you what I drink? What on earth business is it of yours, may I ask . . .

BRIDGET: (*Mimicking her*) What on earth business is it of yours, may I ask?

DAFYDD: All right, girls, that's enough now . . . Call a truce.

LINDA: Snotty little barmaid . . .

TED: Now, now, Linda . . .

BRIDGET: (*Looking dangerous*) Hey . . . hey . . . You watch yourself.

ENID: Now come on, Linda, we're off home now . . .

DAFYDD: That's enough . . .

TED: Now, now, now . . . Linda . . .
(CRISPIN *plays a provocative chord on the piano.*)

BRIDGET: Hey, you. Did you play that? You touch that piano again, you're out that door, all right . . .

CRISPIN: Yes, miss . . . Wasn't me, miss . . .

(LINDA *plonks out several notes on the piano.*)

ENID: Linda! Oh, she is a naughty girl . . .

TED: Now, now, now, Linda. Now, now . . .

BRIDGET: (*Coming round the bar like a tornado*) All right, you. I've had it up to here with you . . .

DAFYDD: Bridget. Easy, Bridget girl. (*To* GUY) God, she doesn't want to get her roused. That girl set up *Carousel* single handed . . .

(BRIDGET *approaches* LINDA.)

BRIDGET: Come on. Out I said.

LINDA: Really? You try and make me leave.

BRIDGET: (*Shoving her*) Out. Out . . .

REBECCA: Peace, children . . .

ENID: (*With her*) Stop them somebody. Someone stop them . . .

TED: (*With them*) Now, now, Linda. Now, now . . .

DAFYDD: (*With them*) I think we've all had our bit of fun and high spirits, people . . .

(CRISPIN, *during this last, steps between the two women and confronts* BRIDGET.)

CRISPIN: Hey . . . Who you pushing around, then?

BRIDGET: Anyone who gets in my way. Want to make something of it?

CRISPIN: Haven't you ever heard that the customer's always right? Haven't you ever heard that, then?

BRIDGET: Not in this pub they aren't. Now sod off . . .

CRISPIN: Language, language . . .

(*He pats her under the chin.* BRIDGET *really goes wild, launching herself at* CRISPIN *with an initial knee to the groin which he narrowly avoids. She follows this with a huge swinging punch, which again he narrowly avoids and which – had it connected – would certainly have laid him out cold. Under this barrage of kicks and punches,* CRISPIN *beats a somewhat undignified retreat towards the door.* LINDA *watches appalled. The others respond with a mixture of amusement and alarm.*)

BRIDGET: (*As this happens*) Go on . . . get out, out, out, out, OUT!

CRISPIN: (*Half amused at this onslaught*) All right, all right, all right. I'm going, I'm going.

(*They both disappear into the street momentarily. Then* BRIDGET *returns triumphantly. She gets a cheer.* LINDA *stalks with dignity to the door.* BRIDGET *with mock politeness holds open the door for her.*)

ENID: (*Apprehensively*) Linda . . .

LINDA: (*Coolly*) Good night.

BRIDGET: Good nate.

(LINDA *goes out.*)

And it is now time, please, so can I have your glasses? Thank you.

(*Mutters and groans of complaint.*)

JARVIS: (*Calling to* GUY) Hey! Scotty. Remind you of Glasgow, eh? Home from home. (*He laughs.*)

DAFYDD: (*Gloomily*) Whenever you're in here you just have to keep saying over to yourself, 'I know it's hell but the beer is good.' That my glass, is it?

GUY: (*Handing him the totally depleted glass.*) Yes. Sorry.

DAFYDD: Oh, well. Bang goes another reason for living. (*He shrugs.*) I hope Bridget hasn't offended that lad. We need him for the show.

GUY: What's he playing?

DAFYDD: Macheath. Well, maybe he wasn't the most ideal choice for the leading role. Temperamentally, anyway. But we had no real choice. Not with Tommy Binns' cartilage problem.

(REBECCA *and* JARVIS *pass them on their way out.* REBECCA *moving with extreme, sedate caution.*)

Goodnight, both.

REBECCA: Goodnight. (*With a glassily charming smile to* GUY) See you tomorrow.

GUY: Yes, indeed . . .

JARVIS: See you the noo. Eh? See you the noo . . . (*He laughs.*)

GUY: (*Laughing*) Yes, yes . . .

REBECCA: (*As they go out*) Are you sure he's Scottish . . . ?

(REBECCA *and* JARVIS *leave.*)

DAFYDD: See you where, did he say?

GUY: The noo.

DAFYDD: It's just round the back. (*He roars with laughter and slaps* GUY *on the shoulder*.) Sorry, Guy, you'll have to bear with my coarse Welsh rugby player's humour . . . Beg your pardon.

GUY: Are you a rugger player?

DAFYDD: God, no. Can't stand the game. Had to play it for seven years. Total misery. But my Dad was a fanatic. One of those. All his language was in terms of rugby, you know. That man's up and under imagery constituted my entire verbal childhood upbringing. Making sure life fed you plenty of good clean ball. Getting women in loose mauls and all that bollocks. God, I was glad to leave home . . .

GUY: Your poor mother . . .

DAFYDD: No, she was all right, she left with me . . .
(TED *and* ENID *pass them*.)
Goodnight, Ted. Enid . . .

ENID: We're going off in search of Linda, Dafydd . . .

TED: She's only a child you see, Dafydd . . .

ENID: (*Almost overlapping him*) She's always been mature, you know . . .

TED: (*Almost overlapping her, in turn*) . . . physically, you know . . .

ENID: . . . physically . . . but emotionally . . .

TED: . . . her emotions are still very far from . . .

ENID: . . . for her age . . .

TED: . . . mature, you see.

ENID: . . . immature, yes.

TED: And we're not happy with this lad at all, Dafydd. I mean we're not . . .

ENID: . . . snobbish at all . . .

TED: . . . class conscious. But he's not right . . .

ENID: . . . he's very wrong . . .

TED: . . . he's a very wild lad . . .

ENID: . . . oh, very wild . . .

TED: . . . and we've got a feeling we know where he'll finish up, don't we, Enid?

ENID: Yes, I'm afraid we do. Only too . . .

TED: . . . too well . . .

29

ENID: . . . too well . . .

(*Mercifully they both run out of steam. Slight pause.*)

DAFYDD: Well. If you find you do have a problem, give me a ring at home.

TED: Thank you, Dafydd . . .

ENID: Thank you very much, Dafydd . . .

DAFYDD: I'll be back there in ten minutes. So. 'Night.

TED: Goodnight.

ENID: Goodnight. I hope you sleep well. (*To* GUY) All through the night. (*She laughs.*)

GUY: Thank you. Goodnight. (*He laughs.*)

(TED *and* ENID *go out.*)

DAFYDD: An effortlessly witty woman is Enid, you'll discover. Listen, we haven't settled this business of casting, have we? Think we ought to settle that now, don't you?

GUY: Yes. That would be nice. Give me something to be getting on with. If I know what I'm playing . . .

BRIDGET: (*Making a threatening move to come round the bar*) Are you two leaving or do I have to throw you out?

DAFYDD: (*Retreating in haste*) No, no, Bridget. We're going. We're going. Have you got your car, by any chance . . . ?

GUY: Yes. Just round the corner . . .

DAFYDD: Well, look, my place is only a couple of streets away. I could give you a script and a cup of cocoa. That suit you?

GUY: Fine. Lead on.

(GUY *and* DAFYDD *leave the pub.* BRIDGET *continues to clear up for a moment. Suddenly,* CRISPIN *is in the doorway. He stands menacingly.* BRIDGET *sees him and tenses, ready for a scrap. Silence.* CRISPIN *advances on her slowly. They stand face to face. With a sudden swift movement he reaches out and grabs her by the back of her head. Their mouths meet in a savage kiss. The scene changes to* DAFYDD's *sitting room. Pleasant and comfortable but small. Certainly too small for* DAFYDD. *A room shared with children. A large, male, home-made rag doll sits on one of the chairs.*)

DAFYDD: (*In a whisper*) Yes . . . As I thought. She'll be in bed. She's not much of a night owl, my wife. Of course the

30

children get her up pretty early . . .

GUY: How many do you have?

DAFYDD: Two. Twin girls.

GUY: (*Indicating doll*) Is that theirs?

DAFYDD: Oh yes – let me take your coat – he's what they call their Other Daddy. Whenever I'm away, they bring him out and pretend it's me. I think it's been left there as a hint by someone this evening. I'll put the kettle on. Won't be a second. If you're cold at all, put the fire on. Personally, I think it's pretty warm, don't you? Wait there . . .

(*He goes out.* GUY *surveys the room. After a moment, he sits and waits patiently. It's obviously quite chilly. Quite suddenly and unexpectedly,* HANNAH *enters. She is in her night things, her face shiny with cream and she is obviously not expecting company.*)

HANNAH: (*Speaking as she enters*) Dafydd, if you want anything to – (*Seeing* GUY) Oh.

GUY: (*Rising*) Hallo, I'm –

HANNAH: Oh, God. Excuse me.

(HANNAH *flees the room.* GUY *stands a little bemused. The following conversation is heard off.*)

HANNAH: (*Off*) Dafydd . . .

DAFYDD: (*Off, cheerfully*) Hallo, darling. Got a little bit held up. Sorry.

HANNAH: (*Off*) You told me you weren't bringing anyone home.

DAFYDD: (*Off*) Yes, I know, I know.

HANNAH: (*Off*) I mean I phoned especially, Dafydd. I phoned and said would you be bringing any of them home tonight . . .

DAFYDD: (*Off, under her*) It was a spur of the moment decision . . .

HANNAH: (*Off*) . . . And you said no, which is why I got ready for bed.

DAFYDD: (*Off*) You can go to bed. You can go to bed.

HANNAH: (*Off*) Not if there's someone here I can't.

DAFYDD: It's all right. This chap doesn't matter.

HANNAH: (*Off*) Who is he?

DAFYDD: (*Off*) He's no one. He's no one important. He's a small-part player, that's all.

HANNAH: (*Off*) I'll get dressed.

DAFYDD: (*Off, calling after her as she departs*) Don't bother. He's not worth getting dressed for. (*Pause.*) God damn it. (*A door slams off. A second later,* DAFYDD *reappears. He is holding a script.*) Here we are. Sorry to keep you. (*Suddenly aware that* GUY *must have heard some of that*) Things are just – heating up out there. By the way, I never asked you. Tea, coffee or cocoa?

GUY: Tea?

DAFYDD: No problem. Now – (*he studies the script*) – I – er – hear you ran into the wife.

GUY: Well . . .

DAFYDD: Or rather she ran into you. (*He laughs.*)

GUY: That's more like it, yes.

DAFYDD: (*Feeling some explanation is due but unable to think of one*) Yes. She's – you know – women . . .

GUY: Yes.

DAFYDD: Never like being taken by surprise, do they? Unless they know what it is in advance. (*He laughs.*) I'd like to surprise you for your birthday, darling, what would you like? Now then. This casting business. I have a feeling, an instinctive feeling in my bones, you know, and I'm not often wrong – sometimes, not often – that you'd make a pretty good Crook-Finger'd Jack. Fancy that, do you? Having a crack at Crook-Finger'd Jack?

GUY: Yes, he sounds pretty interesting . . . yes . . .

DAFYDD: I'll be honest, it's not a vast – you know *The Beggar's Opera* at all – ?

GUY: No. It's one I haven't . . .

DAFYDD: No, well, it's as I say, it's not a vast part. But he does feature. He features pretty strongly really. I mean for the sort of size of part he is. I mean, he's got – what – in terms of speeches – ? (*He flicks the script vaguely.*) Well, he's got probably just the one line in Act Two but he's the sort of character, you know, at the end of an evening, an audience tend to remember quite graphically . . .

GUY: Perhaps that's because of his finger . . .

DAFYDD: (*Failing to see this small joke*) What? No, you see the play's full of these marvellous characters. There are the highwaymen . . . (*savouring the names*) Crook-Finger'd Jack, Jemmy Twitcher, Nimming Ned, Ben Budge, Matt of the Mint . . . (*He reflects.*) Yes, there was the possibility of that character but – my feeling is, as director, that Matt of the Mint could be a little too adventurous for you first time round.

GUY: No, fair enough. I wasn't . . .

DAFYDD: That, of course, is not in any way a reflection on . . .

GUY: No, please, please. I'll be guided by you . . .

DAFYDD: (*Relieved*) Well. Good. Good. I'm giving that particular part to Dr Packer who has, to be fair, had a good deal of experience. Still, it'll only be the first of many for you and us. Hopefully.

GUY: I hope so, too.

DAFYDD: Good. (*Handing* GUY *the script*) You want to take this one?

GUY: Thank you.

DAFYDD: You'll find he comes on around page 32. Then he goes off on page 35, I think. And then I'm thinking seriously about bringing him on again in Act Three. But that's to be confirmed.

GUY: Splendid. Thank you very much.

DAFYDD: Quite a departure for PALOS, this, you know . . .

GUY: PALOS?

DAFYDD: Pendon Amateur Light Operatic Society . . .

GUY: Oh, yes. Sorry. Of course . . .

DAFYDD: Makes a change from *The Student Prince*. Not that I don't . . . But it's good to have a change now and again. I had a lot of opposition in committee over this one, I can tell you. Lot of old die-hards there. Original walk-ons in *Chu Chin Chow*. You know the sort . . . But I'm absolutely convinced that this show – first produced when was it – ? 1728 – it's as entertaining and as vital and as relevant as it

was then . . . Suky Tawdry . . . Dolly Trull . . . Mrs Vixen
. . . Those are the whores and pimps of the town . . .
almost see their faces in their names, can't you? Polly
Peachum. That tells you all you need to know about her,
doesn't it? What an age, eh? What an age. Well, compared
to our own.

GUY: Yes. Yes. Of course, they didn't have any . . .

DAFYDD: I mean, look at us today. Sex shops, I ask you. Can
you imagine Captain Macheath furtively purchasing marital
aids . . . ? What's happening to us, Guy? What's
happening to us, eh? (*Slight pause.*) Sorry, I get a little –
over-enthusiastic occasionally. So I'm told.

GUY: Not at all. Did you ever consider doing the theatre
professionally? I mean, it's just that you seem . . .

DAFYDD: Oh, I was, I was. I was in the profession for some
years.

GUY: Really?

DAFYDD: Oh, yes. I've done my bit.

GUY: As a producer?

DAFYDD: No, no. Acting in those days. I was acting. And a little
bit of stage management, you know.

GUY: Whereabouts?

DAFYDD: (*Vaguely*) Oh, all over. A lot of it in Minehead.

GUY: Oh. Yes.

DAFYDD: Still. That's under the bridge. Respectable solicitor
these days. Well, reasonably. What line are you in, then?

GUY: Oh, I'm –

(*Before he can reply,* HANNAH *enters. She has made herself
more socially presentable now, pretending the earlier encounter
with* GUY *did not occur. She carries a tray with two mugs of
cocoa.* GUY *rises politely.* DAFYDD, *unused to such niceties in
his own home, does so belatedly.*)

HANNAH: Hallo . . .

GUY: Hallo.

DAFYDD: Here she is . . . This is my wife, Hannah.

HANNAH: How do you do?

GUY: How do you do?

DAFYDD: Dearest, this is Mr Jones. Guy Jones.

HANNAH: Hallo.

GUY: Hallo.

DAFYDD: Let me . . . (*He helps her with the tray.*) . . . On here, shall we?

HANNAH: Yes, it'll mark it on there . . . (*To* GUY) Do sit down, please . . . Brrr! It's cold in here. Heating's off.

DAFYDD: Is it? Can't say we'd noticed, had we? Boiling.

HANNAH: I presumed you both wanted cocoa. I saw the tin was out.

DAFYDD: Oh, no. Guy wanted tea. Sorry, love . . .

GUY: It doesn't matter . . .

HANNAH: I can make tea . . .

GUY: No, please, really . . .

DAFYDD: Tea's no trouble . . .

GUY: No, this is perfect. Please.

HANNAH: Well. If you're quite sure.

GUY: I'm just as happy with this.

(*Slight pause.*)

HANNAH: Well, I'll leave you both to it, then.

DAFYDD: Don't go, don't go . . .

HANNAH: If you want to talk business . . .

DAFYDD: No, we've finished. Sit down for a second.

GUY: (*Smiling*) Please.

HANNAH: Well. Only if I'm not in the way. (*She sits.*)

DAFYDD: Anyway. Hardly call it business, could we?

HANNAH: Oh?

DAFYDD: Guy's going to be giving us his Crook-Finger'd Jack.

HANNAH: Sorry?

DAFYDD: Our missing brigand. He's just joined us.

HANNAH: Oh. Wonderful.

DAFYDD: Think he'll make a good Jack, do you, Hannah? Think he'll make a highwayman?

HANNAH: Well. Possibly . . .

DAFYDD: Oh dear, Guy. She doesn't sound too convinced. Doesn't he convince you?

HANNAH: Yes. I just think he looks a bit handsome for a highwayman. (*She smiles nervously.*)

DAFYDD: (*Roaring with laughter*) Well, I don't know what you

35

say to that, Guy, I really don't. What do you say to that?

GUY: I don't really know.

    (*He smiles.* DAFYDD's *laughter subsides. A silence.*)

DAFYDD: Maybe we can give him an eyepatch.

HANNAH: Yes . . .

    (*They laugh. Another silence.*)

DAFYDD: Are the girls all right?

HANNAH: Yes. They're asleep.

DAFYDD: Gwinny stopped coughing?

HANNAH: Oh yes, I gave her the linctus.

DAFYDD: Good. Good. (*Pause.*) Good.

HANNAH: (*To* GUY) We have twin girls.

GUY: Yes . . .

HANNAH: Gwynneth who's got a cold. And Myfanwy who's just getting over it . . . They just go in circles.

GUY: Nice names.

HANNAH: Yes. Dafydd's mother chose them.

DAFYDD: With our help.

GUY: Ah . . .

DAFYDD: Everything's Welsh in this house . . .

HANNAH: Except me, that is.

DAFYDD: Except her, that is. She was made in Middlesex.

GUY: (*Rather over-reacting*) Oh, really? Middlesex.

HANNAH: Yes. Are you from Middlesex, then?

GUY: No.

HANNAH: Oh.

DAFYDD: He's from Leeds. Aren't you?

GUY: That's right.

HANNAH: Oh. Leeds, yes . . . Is your wife local?

DAFYDD: No, dearest, he hasn't got a wife . . .

HANNAH: No?

GUY: No, she . . . She died, recently.

HANNAH: Oh, dear.

DAFYDD: Oh dear, I didn't know that. Accident, was it?

GUY: No. Not really, it was . . . (*He searches for words.*)

DAFYDD: Deliberate. (*He laughs.*)

HANNAH: (*Fiercely*) Dafydd . . .

DAFYDD: Sorry, sorry. I do beg your pardon. I'm sorry, Guy.

GUY: That's quite all right . . .

HANNAH: He's always doing that.

GUY: She was ill for some time, actually . . .

HANNAH: Oh, dear. How long's she . . . How long's she – been now?

GUY: Just over a year . . .

HANNAH: Ah.

DAFYDD: Ah . . .

GUY: It took me a little time, obviously, to adjust . . .

HANNAH: . . . yes, it would . . .

GUY: Still, eventually I decided it was high time I took a grip on things and got out and about again. Which is why I took the plunge and wrote to David . . .

DAFYDD: (*Correcting him*) Dafydd . . .

GUY: (*Attempting the correct pronunciation*) Dafydd . . .

DAFYDD: Nearly. (*Spelling it out slowly*) Da–fydd . . .

GUY: Da–fydd . . .

HANNAH: Oh, really. It's near enough.

DAFYDD: Near enough is not enough . . .

HANNAH: It's bad enough as it is. How do you fancy standing in the Dry Cleaners trying to pronounce your own surname?

DAFYDD: (*The full Welsh*) Llewellyn. What could be simpler? Llewellyn . . .

HANNAH: You work locally, though, do you?

GUY: Yes, I'm with BLM, actually.

DAFYDD: BLM? Over on Western Estate?

GUY: That's right . . .

DAFYDD: The big boys, eh?

GUY: Well, they are, I'm not.

HANNAH: What do they do, BLM? I've always meant to ask.

GUY: Well . . .

DAFYDD: That's a difficult one to answer, eh, Guy?

GUY: Just a bit . . .

HANNAH: I mean, what do they do? Do they make anything?

DAFYDD: (*Laughing*) Vast profits mostly . . . Right?

GUY: Right. (*He laughs.*)

HANNAH: Oh well, don't tell me if you don't want to . . .

GUY: We're a multi-national company that's become extremely diversified . . .

DAFYDD: Diversified, dearest. That means they're into all sorts of different –

HANNAH: (*Tetchily*) Yes, I know, I know . . .

DAFYDD: All right . . .

HANNAH: I know what diversify means.

GUY: (*A fraction embarrassed*) And so it's a bit difficult to pin down. Certainly it is from my limited viewpoint. In a rather small local branch in a rather obscure department called Alternative Forward Costing. In which I am a very small cog indeed.

HANNAH: I'm impressed anyway.

DAFYDD: It's interesting you should be in BLM because –– (*In the hall the phone rings.*)

HANNAH: Who can that be . . . ? (*She starts to rise.*)

DAFYDD: (*Rising*) I'll go, I'll go. It could be Ted . . .

HANNAH: Oh, is it Linda trouble again?

DAFYDD: (*As he goes*) Yes, as usual. As usual . . . (DAFYDD *goes out.*)

HANNAH: It's these friends of ours, they have this daughter that they absolutely dote over. And of course she just takes terrible advantage of them all the time . . .

GUY: Yes, I met them.

HANNAH: Did you? Yes. She's a real headache for them. She set fire to all her mother's clothes, you know . . .

GUY: Set fire to them?

HANNAH: Yes. Enid wasn't in them at the time but it was everything she had in the world except what she was standing up in. They both came home from a meeting of the Civic Society and her wardrobe was ablaze.

GUY: Heavens.

HANNAH: Mind you, I can't help thinking, in some ways, they brought it on themselves. I hope ours will turn out all right. Do you have children, Mr – ?

GUY: Guy, please. No. My wife wasn't able to have any. She – wasn't very strong . . .

HANNAH: Shame. Do you miss her a lot?

GUY: (*As if considering the question for the first time*) Yes. Yes, I do. Very much.

HANNAH: That's nice. For her, I mean. Of course not for you. I'd like to think I'd be missed.

GUY: You?

HANNAH: Yes.

GUY: Why? (*An awful thought.*) You're not . . . ?

HANNAH: Oh, no. No, I'm right as rain. I think. So far as I know. It's just I sometimes wonder, I suppose a lot of us do probably, whether if I – you know – died, people would really . . . Silly really, isn't it?

GUY: I'm sure you'd be missed.

HANNAH: Maybe.

GUY: By David – Dafydd. And your children.

HANNAH: Yes, possibly the children would. For a few more years, anyway. I don't know about Dafydd. Now he *is* missed. You see that big doll there? Every time Dafydd's out of the house for more than 20 minutes the girls insist it's brought out. Then all their games revolve round that wretched doll. Tea with Daddy-doll and walks with Daddy-doll and supper with Daddy-doll and bed with Daddy-doll . . . Well, I've stopped them taking it to bed with them now. I did think that was getting too much of a good thing. Of course, Dafydd thinks it's terribly funny. I suppose it is quite flattering for him, really. The trouble is, my family are under the impression that there's a female counterpart to that thing that runs round the house after them. Only it happens to be me. Hooray for Mummy-doll.

(*Slight pause.*)

Heavens. I haven't talked like this for years. I am sorry. It's very boring of me.

GUY: (*Gently*) No.

HANNAH: No?

GUY: No.

(*He smiles at her.* HANNAH, *uncertainly at first and then more warmly, smiles back at* GUY. *As they gaze at each other,* DAFYDD *returns from the phone to break the spell.*)

39

DAFYDD: (*As he enters*) That was Enid. They got home and found Linda in bed.

(HANNAH *is about to say something*.)

Yes, that's what I asked. And the answer is no. Fast asleep on her own. So, false alarm. They still have a daughter and more important we still have a Lucy Lockit. What's been going on in here? Anything I should know about?

HANNAH: I think it's my bedtime, if you'll excuse me . . .

GUY: (*Looking at his watch*) Oh, Lord, yes. I must be . . .

DAFYDD: Don't go on my account. I'm a late one myself . . .

GUY: No, it really is . . .

DAFYDD: (*Going out briefly*) I'll fetch your coat, then.

GUY: (*To* HANNAH) Thank you very much for your hospitality . . .

HANNAH: Not much of that. You didn't even drink your cocoa.

GUY: Another time, perhaps.

(DAFYDD *returns and helps* GUY *into his coat*.)

Thank you. I hope, in any case, I'll see you again before too long.

DAFYDD: What her? You're talking about Hannah, you mean? You'll see her tomorrow night.

GUY: (*Pleased*) Oh, really?

DAFYDD: Didn't she tell you she's in the show? She's our Polly Peachum, aren't you, love? (*He cuffs her affectionately*.)

GUY: Oh. I see. Good Lord.

HANNAH: (*As she leaves with the tray*) I look better in the mornings. Usually. (*She laughs*.) See you tomorrow.

GUY: Goodnight. (*He stares after her somewhat as of a man enchanted*.)

DAFYDD: (*A man with his mind on more serious things*) Listen, Guy . . . a word before you go . . .

GUY: Yes?

DAFYDD: This coincidence of your working for BLM. It could be quite opportune. The point is, I'm acting for a client at the moment who's involved in purchasing a couple of acres of wasteland. Small stuff. Nothing very exciting. Except for two things. One, the land is actually slap bang adjoining your premises –

GUY: Oh, round the back there, you mean?

DAFYDD: Yes, the old sports field. Used to be a sports field. Second, and this is only hearsay, rumour has it that you boys are shortly planning to expand. Any truth in that, do you know?

GUY: No, I don't . . . Not so far as I know . . .

DAFYDD: Only, of course, if you are, then of course the land in question could suddenly be worth a bit. Do you follow?

GUY: Yes, I do see.

DAFYDD: Depending of course on how many people get to know about it. I mean, putting it in plainer words, if the chap who's selling it doesn't know, whereas we who are buying it do know – then we could be getting a bargain. But you've no definite knowledge yourself?

GUY: No, as I say, not that's come to my ears. I could ask . . .

DAFYDD: Well, tactfully if you do. Don't want to disturb things, do we? Of course, if you could help, there'd – there'd be some arrangement, no doubt . . .

GUY: Oh, there'd be no need for . . .

DAFYDD: Oh, yes, yes. Fair's fair. Fair's fair . . .

GUY: Yes. Though I suppose if we were being really fair, we really ought to warn the person who's selling the land.

DAFYDD: Oh, I don't think that's on.

GUY: No?

DAFYDD: If I did that, I'd be betraying my own client, wouldn't I? Wouldn't be ethical.

GUY: I see.

DAFYDD: No. It's up to this other fellow's solicitor to warn him. Not me. Anyway. Keep your ear to the ground.

(*He steers* GUY *towards the front door.*)

GUY: I will certainly.

DAFYDD: But remember, mum's the word.

GUY: Oh, yes, rather. Goodnight then. See you tomorrow.

DAFYDD: You betcher. Seven o'clock. And we're really going to get cracking, I can tell you. You won't see that stage for dust.

GUY: (*Moving away*) Right . . .

DAFYDD: (*Calling after him as* GUY *goes*) Better bring your racing skates . . .

(DAFYDD *stands in the doorway for a second, savouring the night air. A man well pleased with his evening's achievements. As he stands there, lights up on* TED. *He is in full evening dress, holding his script.*)

TED: (*As Peachum, singing*)
A Fox may steal your Hens, Sir,
A Whore your Health and Pence, Sir,
Your Daughter rob your Chest, Sir,
Your Wife may steal your Rest, Sir,
A Thief your Goods and Plate.
But this is all but picking,
With Rest, Pence, Chest and Chicken;
It ever was decreed, Sir,
If Lawyer's Hand is fee'd, Sir,
He steals your whole Estate.

(*Lights come up on the full rehearsal area. Also on stage now are* DAFYDD, *prowling the auditorium watching* TED. GUY *sitting to one side, absorbed and eager to learn.* BRIDGET *sitting with the prompt script, slightly bored and restless. And away in another corner* IAN, *at present reading the evening paper and taking no perceptible interest in proceedings. As the song finishes,* TED *consults his script, makes to sit, changes his mind and exits offstage. As he does so* ENID, *as Mrs Peachum, and* HANNAH, *as Polly, come on, also holding their scripts.* ENID *is also in evening dress.*)

HANNAH: (*Reading, as Polly*) 'Twas only Nimming Ned. He brought in a Damask Window-Curtain, a Hoop Petticoat, a Pair Of Silver Candlesticks, a Perriwig, and one Silk Stocking, from the Fire that happen'd last Night.

(*She stops at the end of her speech. Both women look up expecting* TED *to reply, but he has gone.*)

DAFYDD: (*Yelling*) Go on, go on, go on. Don't stop again, for God's sake. We're ten days behind as it is.

HANNAH: We can't go on.

DAFYDD: Who's next, Bridget? Keep your eye on the script, girl. Who speaks next?

BRIDGET: Ted.

DAFYDD: Ted? Well, where the hell is Ted? He's just walked off

42

the stage. Where's he gone to? (*Yelling*) Ted!

(TED *returns a little apprehensively.*)

TED: Did you want me, Dafydd?

DAFYDD: Ted, love, there is no earthly point in leaving the stage when you're in the middle of a scene, now is there?

TED: (*Consulting his script*) Oh. Don't I go off? I thought I went off . . .

(ENID *and* HANNAH *go to* TED's *rescue, showing him where he is in the script.*)

HANNAH: . . . I don't think you go off till there, Ted . . .

ENID: . . . there, dear, you see. Not till there . . .

TED: . . . Oh, I see. There. I thought it was there . . .

DAFYDD: (*On the move with impatience, as he passes* GUY *over this last.*) Unbelievable this, isn't it? Unbelievable. Ten days we've been at this. Ten days. And where are we – ? Page 15 or something . . .

HANNAH: (*To* DAFYDD) We've got it now. It was a mistake.

TED: My mistake. Sorry, everyone. I shouldn't have gone off . . .

DAFYDD: Well, I'm sure you were only expressing in actions, Ted, what will by this stage be the heartfelt wish of the entire audience . . .

TED: (*Laughing, nervously*) Yes, yes . . .

DAFYDD: Those that won't already have dozed off, or died of old age . . .

HANNAH: (*In a warning tone*) Dafydd . . .

DAFYDD: Why are you dressed like a cinema manager, anyway, Ted?

HANNAH: It's their dinner dance, Dafydd. They were due there an hour ago. You promised to release them early.

DAFYDD: Oh, terrific. My whole rehearsal grinds to a halt because of a Co-op staff dance, does it?

TED: No hurry, Dafydd. No hurry. We didn't want the dinner.

DAFYDD: All right. Let's get on. (*Fiercely*) On, on . . .

HANNAH: (*Picking it up again, as Polly*) . . . one silk stocking, from the Fire that happen'd last Night.

TED: (*As Peachum*) There is not a Fellow that is cleverer in his way, and saves more Goods out of the . . .

BRIDGET: That's cut.

TED: Sorry?

ENID: I think we cut that, dear . . .

DAFYDD: (*Storming on to the stage*) Ted, that is cut. That was cut two days ago . . .

TED: I'm sorry. I didn't have it . . .

DAFYDD: You don't have anything, Ted. That's your trouble, man. You don't have any ability, you don't have any intelligence, you don't have one single scrap of artistic sensibility and most important of all you don't even have a bloody pencil.

HANNAH: Dafydd . . .

DAFYDD: (*Wrenching TED's script from his hands*) That is cut . . . (*Stabbing his finger at the page*) That is cut and *that* is cut. And the whole – (*wrestling with the script*) – sodding thing is cut. (*He rips TED's script in several pieces.*)
(*Breathless*) There! That make it any easier for you? You boneheaded – tortoise . . .
(TED *stands shattered. He opens his mouth to reply and finds himself unable to do so. He leaves the stage rather swiftly, one suspects on the verge of tears.*)

ENID: Oh, Dafydd . . . You really are – sometimes. You really are . . . There was no need for that . . .
(ENID *goes off after* TED.)

DAFYDD: God, it's hot in here, isn't it? Anybody else find it too hot?

HANNAH: (*In a low voice*) That was unforgivable, Dafydd. To Ted of all people. Absolutely unforgivable . . .
(*She picks up the torn script, angrily shouting*) And these scripts are supposed to go back. I hope you realize that.
(HANNAH *goes off after* TED *and* ENID.)

DAFYDD: (*Searching for fresh allies*) Dear old Guy. Dear old Guy. You sitting there quietly picking up some tips, are you?

GUY: (*Smiling*) Yes, yes . . .

DAFYDD: I'm afraid this is what we term the amateur syndrome, Guy. When the crunch comes, they can't take the pressure,

44

you see. Want to be off to their dinner dances. God, there are times when I come close to wishing I was back at Minehead.

GUY: I wondered – if you had a minute – I wondered if I could ask you about Crook-Finger'd Jack . . .

DAFYDD: Who?

GUY: My part. Crook-Finger'd Jack . . .

DAFYDD: Oh, Crook-Finger'd Jack. Yes. What about him?

GUY: It's just that I've been thinking about it over the past few days, you know, and I wondered whether you'd like him with a finger.

DAFYDD: A what?

GUY: A finger. (*He holds up his hand and demonstrates.*) Something like that. (*Pause.*) Or maybe – the other hand. (*He changes hands. Pause. Offering* DAFYDD *an alternating choice of hands*) Which do you think?

DAFYDD: (*Snapping out of his reverie*) Yes. Do you think we could leave that for a day or two longer, Guy, old boy? I've one or two rather more pressing matters . . .

GUY: Oh yes, yes. Of course. Sorry.

BRIDGET: I'm going to make some tea. (*She starts to get up slowly.*)

DAFYDD: Splendid, my love, excellent . . .

(REBECCA *and* FAY *come on, followed by* LINDA. *All in their coats.* BRIDGET *goes off.*)

REBECCA: Dafydd. We come to you as a deputation. We have been sitting backstage in that ghastly smelly little kitchen for the best part of two weeks . . .

DAFYDD: All right, all right, all right. Don't you start . . .

REBECCA: We're not being unreasonable, Dafydd. All we want to know is, will you be needing us this evening or will you not? If not, fair enough. Only some of us have nice comfy homes we'd prefer to be in . . .

DAFYDD: Go on, go home. Go home to your nice, comfy little homes. Go on, bugger off, the lot of you.

(*A glacial moment.* BRIDGET *crosses and goes off.*)

REBECCA: Well, I am certainly not staying after that. Not to listen to language like that.

DAFYDD: Goodbye.

REBECCA: And furthermore, I shall be having a word with the Committee about this whole business. Do you realize Mr Washbrook is in tears out there?

DAFYDD: So am I . . .

REBECCA: (*To* FAY) Are you coming, Fay?

FAY: No point in staying here, is there?

(REBECCA *sweeps out.* FAY *goes to follow.*)

(*To* IAN, *indicating* GUY) We're going over the road, all right?

IAN: Right. (*He starts to fold up his paper.*)

FAY: (*Seeing* GUY *is watching her, brightly, to him*) You coming for a drink?

GUY: Probably. In a minute.

FAY: Good. See you over there.

(FAY *goes out after* REBECCA. LINDA *trails after them.* BRIDGET *returns with a pint of milk.*)

DAFYDD: Linda, is your Crispin around anywhere, do you know?

LINDA: I don't know where he is. Why should I know?

DAFYDD: Well, have you seen him?

LINDA: No, I have not seen him and I have no wish to see him, thank you very much . . . (*At* BRIDGET) I should ask her.

DAFYDD: Oh, God. (*To* BRIDGET) Do you know where he is?

BRIDGET: Where I left him, probably.

DAFYDD: Where?

BRIDGET: In my bed. Asleep.

(LINDA *glares furiously and goes.* BRIDGET *goes out, looking pleased. She passes* TED *and* ENID, *now in their coats, who both cross the stage on their way out. Both are very tearful and snuffling softly.* DAFYDD *watches them.*)

DAFYDD: (*Rather lamely*) Goodnight . . . folks. Have a great – evening, won't you? (*After they've gone, filled with remorse*) Oh, God. (*He sits.*)

(*Almost immediately,* HANNAH *returns.*)

HANNAH: I told the Washbrooks they could go. Phone for you, backstage. Dr Packer. Says it's urgent.

DAFYDD: More problems . . . more problems . . .
(DAFYDD *goes off.* HANNAH *catches* GUY's *eye briefly and smiles.* IAN *intercepts the look.* HANNAH *goes after* DAFYDD. IAN *now also moves to the door.*)

IAN: Right. After that exhausting night's work, I feel like some refreshment. (*To* GUY) You coming?

GUY: I was just going to run my line a couple of times. I've got one or two ideas I'd like to try . . .

IAN: (*Dryly*) Well, don't get stale, will you? Two months to go yet. (*He starts to move off.*)

GUY: (*Calling him back*) I say . . . (*Demonstrating his Crook-Finger'd Jack stance again*) Do you think this is too obvious? Crook-Finger'd Jack . . .

IAN: Can't be too obvious for Dafydd. Did you see his *Sound of Music*?

GUY: No.

IAN: He had them all on trampolines.

GUY: Heavens.

IAN: Bloody hills were alive, I can tell you. So were the front stalls. Once they got in their costumes they couldn't control the bounce, you see. Screaming nuns crashing down on the punters. Three broken legs and one of them concussed on the spot bar. Probably some still up there for all we know . . .

GUY: (*Not knowing quite whether to believe this*) Yes. I think I'll try it without the finger to start with . . .

IAN: By the way . . . ?

GUY: Mm?

IAN: We'd like to invite you round some evening. To our place.

GUY: Oh. That's very nice. Thank you.

IAN: I don't know if you've got anyone you'd care to bring. I understand you're not married any more . . .

GUY: No, my wife was –

IAN: Yes. Well. I daresay you've got a friend. Or someone. Eh?

GUY: Yes, I think I could probably find a friend, yes.

IAN: (*Smiling*) Female, of course.

GUY: Oh yes. Of course. Don't want to spoil your numbers.

IAN: No, no. (*Pause. Uncertain whether* GUY *has got the message*)

The point is Fay and I, we – well, you've probably gathered by now she's pretty – gregarious.

GUY: Yes.

IAN: And she likes to meet new people. All the time. And frankly, so do I. So it all tends to work out. If you follow me.

GUY: (*Who doesn't.*) Well, that's splendid. When were you thinking?

IAN: Is Friday OK for you?

GUY: Friday, yes.

IAN: We can have a bit of fun. (*He laughs.*)

GUY: Splendid.

IAN: Don't forget your friend, though.

GUY: I won't.

IAN: (*As he leaves*) And I'd like to talk to you about your job sometime. I'm very interested in that.

(IAN *goes.*)

GUY: (*Puzzled*) Really?

(*Realizing he is alone, he decides to experiment.*)

GUY: (*As Jack*) Where shall we find such another set . . . (*He breaks off.*) No. (*Trying again*) Where shall we find such another Set of Practical Philosophers who to a Man are above the Fear of Death? Ha! Ha! Ho. (*He tries again.*)

(JARVIS *has entered from backstage, on his way home. He watches him.* GUY *stops, rather embarrassed as he becomes aware of* JARVIS.)

JARVIS: Hey! The noo. That's what I like to see. A man practising his craft. I have a story about that. Will interest you. When I first went into t'firm as an apprentice lad – no matter I were boss's son I started on t'shop floor – the first day there the foreman says – big fellow he was – sweep that floor spotless, lad. Spotless. I want to eat my dinner off that floor. All right? And I sort of half swept it, you know, like you might. And when he comes back he said, what's this then, he says? And he bends down and he picks up this handful of sawdust that I'd missed, like. Under the bench. And he says, you're not expecting me to eat me dinner off

48

this floor then, are you? He says, I'd like to see you try it, my lad, he says. And he tells me, sit down, and he fetches a gummy-bowl and spoon from rack and he makes me eat all that sawdust. Just as it is. Every scrap.

GUY: Heavens.

JARVIS: Nothing on it. Nor milk nor sugar. Raw sawdust. And it's the same like that every day for three months. No matter I were t'boss's son. Those lads down in that shop, they taught me the hard way with mouthfuls of sawdust.

GUY: Tough life.

JARVIS: Oh, aye. Mind you, a while later, me Dad had his stroke and I took over t'firm. I went down that shop, first thing I did, and sacked every bloody one of 'em. But I learnt the trade. I were grateful to 'em for that.

GUY: Jolly good.

JARVIS: Keep at it. Practise your gestures. They all had gestures, you know . . .

GUY: I will, I will.

JARVIS: And another thing. Don't put on that fancy voice for it. Use your natural accent. That's what I do. Besides, he could be a Scotty. Couldn't he? A Scotty.

GUY: True, only . . .

JARVIS: Stick up for thissen then, lad. Stick up for thissen. People won't think the less of you for it, you know.

GUY: Yes. Right. Thank you.

(JARVIS *goes out.* GUY *briefly tries his role with a thick Scots accent. More for his own amusement than anything.*)
Wherrr shall we find such anotherrr wee Set o' Practical Phullussupherrs. Jummy. Whoo to a man are above the ferr of dea' . . .

(HANNAH *comes on with two cups of tea. She catches some of his performance.*)

HANNAH: I brought you some tea.

GUY: Oh, thank you.

HANNAH: Dafydd's on the phone. Another crisis, I think.

GUY: Ah, well.

HANNAH: You – er – you weren't thinking of playing him like that, were you? With that funny accent?

GUY: No, no. That was just an – experiment.

HANNAH: Oh, good. Only I thought you nearly had it right yesterday. With the limp. The slight one.

GUY: Yes. Maybe I'll stick to that. I think it's waiting all this time to rehearse the scene, it makes you – anxious . . .

HANNAH: Yes. He'll get to you eventually.

GUY: Oh, yes, I'm sure.

HANNAH: (*More to herself*) God knows when, though. (*Producing her script*) I wondered if you'd mind awfully hearing my lines again.

GUY: No. Not at all. (*He takes her script.*) Where would you . . . ?

HANNAH: Just from the top of the page.

GUY: OK.

HANNAH: (*As Polly*) And are *you* as fond as ever, my Dear?

GUY: (*Reading, as Macheath*) Suspect my Honour, my Courage, suspect any thing but my Love. – May my Pistols miss Fire, and my Mare slip her Shoulder while I am pursu'd, if I ever forsake thee!

HANNAH: (*As Polly*) Nay, my Dear, I have no Reason to doubt you, for I find in the Romance you lent me . . .
(*She hesitates.* GUY *nods encouragingly.*)
. . . you lent me, none of the great Heroes was ever false in Love.
(*She smiles at* GUY. GUY *smiles at her.* DAFYDD *enters. His head is bowed.* HANNAH *and* GUY *wrench their attention away from each other.* DAFYDD *solemnly beats his head against a piece of furniture.*)

HANNAH: (*To* DAFYDD) Problems?

DAFYDD: One or two. Dr Packer has just phoned to inform me that faced as he is with the alternative of either reorganizing the new hospital rostas entirely or relinquishing the role of Matt of the Mint, he has reluctantly decided on the latter course of action. So there you are. Once again, as my father would put it, we are beaten by the bounce.

HANNAH: What are you going to do?

DAFYDD: How the hell should I know?

HANNAH: (*Softly, nodding in Guy's direction.*) Guy . . .

DAFYDD: (*Sotto*) What?

HANNAH: Guy.

DAFYDD: Guy?

HANNAH: Yes.

DAFYDD: You think so?

HANNAH: Of course.

DAFYDD: (*Turning to* GUY, *extending a hand*) Guy . . .

GUY: Yes?

DAFYDD: I think you are to be cast in the role of saviour. Can you do it? Matt of the Mint?

GUY: Oh.

DAFYDD: For me? For us all?

GUY: Well. I'll have a go.

DAFYDD: Thank you. Thank you.

HANNAH: Super.

DAFYDD: (*Brightening*) Splendid. Well, what do you say? A drink to celebrate?

GUY: Well, why not?

DAFYDD: I'll get them in. I'll get them in. (*Moving to the door*) But tomorrow, remember, we work . . .

GUY: Er . . .

DAFYDD: Yes?

GUY: What about Crook-Finger'd Jack?

DAFYDD: What about him?

GUY: Only, I'd just learnt him. I wondered if . . .

DAFYDD: Forget Crook-Finger'd Jack, boy. You're Matt of the Mint. You're a star now. Nearly.

(DAFYDD *goes.*)

HANNAH: I'm so thrilled for you. Well done.

(*Impetuously, she kisses him. As it turns out, it is a far more serious kiss than either of them intended.* GUY *eventually releases* HANNAH. *He moves to the door, looking back at her. She looks at him. Finally, he leaves without a further word. As this occurs, the introduction is heard to the next song. The lights come up on* ENID, *whilst also remaining on* HANNAH.)

ENID: (*As Mrs Peachum, sings*)

O, Polly you might have toy'd and kiss'd,

By keeping Men off you keep them on.

HANNAH: (*As Polly, sings*) But he so teaz'd me,
And he so pleas'd me,
What I did you must have done.

ENID *and* HANNAH: (*Together*)
But he so teaz'd thee/me
And he so pleas'd thee/me
What you/I did I/you must have done.
(*The lights at once crossfade again and we are in*
FAY's *sitting room. She is dressed to kill.* FAY *holds two exotic*
drinks.)

FAY: (*Calling*) We're in here . . .

GUY: (*Off*) Right.

FAY: (*Calling*) Can you find it all right? Light switch is just
inside the door.
(*She listens. Hears nothing. Assumes all is well. She puts the*
drinks down on the table and checks her already faultless
appearance in a mirror. GUY *enters.*)

GUY: Sorry. At last.

FAY: (*Indicating his drink*) Help yourself.

GUY: Thank you. (*He takes his drink.*)

FAY: Do tell me if it's too strong, won't you? I can never tell.

GUY: (*Going to drink*) No, I'm sure this will be absolutely – (*He*
nearly chokes as he drinks but controls himself.) That's –
perfect, yes.

FAY: Ian's just popped out. To get some more tequila. I'm
afraid we're hooked on it, these days.

GUY: Oh, yes?

FAY: Have you been there?

GUY: Sorry?

FAY: Mexico.

GUY: No. No. Not Mexico . . .

FAY: Glorious. Parts of it. If you dodge the poverty.

GUY: Ah.

FAY: So. You're the first.

GUY: Yes. (*Looking round*) Yes. Looks like it.

FAY: I'm all right, then, anyway.

GUY: Yes?

FAY: I've got you. (*She laughs.*)

GUY: Yes, yes. (*Pause.*) I suppose that means I'm all right as well then. (*He laughs.*)

FAY: (*Laughing with him*) Very true, yes.
(*Pause.*)

GUY: (*Indicating the walls*) Nice pictures.

FAY: (*Vaguely*) We find them quite stimulating.

GUY: Yes. She's going it a bit, that one up there, isn't she?

FAY: Yes. What about him behind you, then?

GUY: (*Turning in his chair and then with obvious shock*) Oh, good Lord. Yes. (*Studying the picture*) Good Lord.

FAY: We have to take them down when Ian's mother comes to stay . . .

GUY: Yes, I can see she'd probably . . .

FAY: Wait till you see what we've got in the bedroom. (*She laughs.*)

GUY: (*Laughing inordinately*) Yes. Wow. Yes. (*Pause.*) You look very nice.

FAY: Thank you. So do you.

GUY: (*Straightening his tie*) Ah.

FAY: Do you want to take that off?

GUY: No, no. No. That's OK.

FAY: I love men in ties . . .

GUY: Oh, yes? (*Pause.*) You'd like it in our office then. It's full of them.
(*Pause.*)

FAY: Look. I might as well say this early on. Then we can relax and enjoy ourselves. If there's anything you particularly like or positively dislike, you will say, won't you?

GUY: Oh no, no. I'm not at all fussy, never have been. I take just what's put in front of me.

FAY: I mean, as far as I'm concerned, don't worry. I'm very easy. I don't think there's anything. Anything at all. Well, I suppose if it was excessively cruel or painful . . . I would draw the line.

GUY: Oh, yes, yes. (*He considers.*) You mean like veal, for instance.

53

FAY: Veal.

GUY: Veal, you know . . .

FAY: No. I don't think I've tried that.

GUY: You haven't?

FAY: No. Something new. How exciting. I can't wait. Veal. How do you spell it?

GUY: – Er . . . V–E–A–L . . .

FAY: You mean the same as the meat? What's it stand for?

GUY: No idea . . .

FAY: Very Exciting And Lascivious . . . (*She laughs.*) No? Viciously Energetic And Lingering . . . (*They both laugh.*)

GUY: Vomitmaking Especially At Lunchtime . . . (FAY *screams with laughter.*)

FAY: (*Recovering, glancing at her watch*) Your friend's late . . .

GUY: Yes. She is. I'm beginning to get a bit worried. I would have picked her up in the car only she's very independent and she does like to make her own way.

FAY: Why not?

GUY: Quite.

FAY: Has she got far to come?

GUY: No, only a bus ride. From Wellfield Flats.

FAY: Oh, yes. I know. Near the park?

GUY: That's it.

FAY: Wellfield Flats. Aren't those for old people?

GUY: That's right.

FAY: Oh, I see. She works there, does she? As a nurse?

GUY: No, no. She lives there.

FAY: Lives there?

GUY: Yes. Only – well, it's rather tricky. She's a proud old soul and she always hates it when people know she lives at Wellfield. So, if you could try not to mention it, I'd be grateful. You know what they're like at that age . . .

FAY: What age?

GUY: Well, she doesn't let on but my guess is early seventies . . .

FAY: Seventies?

GUY: But you'd never know it. She's up and down flights of

54

stairs like nobody's business. She nursed my wife
through a lot of her illness. I've always been grateful to her
for . . .

(*He tails off.* FAY *is weeping with laughter.*)

You all right?

FAY: Yes, yes . . . (*Recovering a fraction*) And she's coming
here? Tonight?

GUY: Well, I hope so . . .

FAY: I can't wait to see Ian's face . . .

GUY: Ian?

FAY: Dear God, this is wonderful . . . I love you. I love you.

GUY: You needn't worry about the pictures. She's very
broadminded. She's a game old bird, she really is. You'll
like her.

FAY: (*Re-composing herself*) I'm sure. I'm sure.

GUY: (*More dubious*) I hope Ian will get on with her but . . .

(*This starts* FAY *laughing again. She lies on the sofa and flails
her legs.*)

(*Confused*) Sorry, I'm not quite with all this I'm . . .

(FAY *sits up suddenly and listens.*)

FAY: Shh. He's back. Listen. Don't tell him about your friend.
Keep her as a surprise.

GUY: A surprise?

FAY: Please . . .

GUY: All right. Why?

(IAN *enters brandishing a Tequila bottle.*)

IAN: All over the bloody place. Driven five miles for this –
Hiya, Guy – Hallo, doll. You going to fix us one . . . ?

FAY: Sure. (*Taking the bottle*) Guy? Another one?

GUY: Well, if it could be not quite so –

FAY: Sure . . . (*She gathers up both their glasses.*)

IAN: Well, where's your friend, then?

GUY: (*With a glance at* FAY) Oh, she's . . . she's . . . coming
shortly.

(FAY *gives a stifled squeak of laughter.*)

IAN: What's the joke?

FAY: Nothing. Nothing . . .

IAN: There is someone else coming, I take it?

FAY: (*Going out*) Oh. Yes. Definitely someone else coming . . .
(FAY *goes out. Her laughter is heard ringing down the hall.*)

IAN: How many's she had, then?

GUY: No idea.

IAN: (*Settling*) Like the pictures?

GUY: Yes, I've been admiring them. Amazing.

IAN: (*Indicating one particular picture*) Fay can do that, you
know.

GUY: (*With disbelief*) Can she really? How incredible.

IAN: One of the few women I know who can. You must get her
to show you. (*Briskly*) Now, just before things start hotting
up and getting out of hand – Could I just clear up this little
business matter?

GUY: Of course, of course.

IAN: I won't beat about the bush. My partner and I have this
little building firm, as you probably know, and we're
contemplating buying a small piece of land which, as it
happens, adjoins your factory.

GUY: Yes, I know the piece. It so . . .

IAN: Good. Well, there is a rumour – (*Laughing*) – isn't there
always? – that BLM may be intending to develop their
existing premises. In which case, of course, the land in
question could become a little more expensive. You follow?

GUY: Yes. As a matter –

IAN: All I'm asking is, is the rumour true?

GUY: Well, all I can give you is the same answer I gave Dafydd.
I honestly have no idea, but I'll try and find out. I've had
no luck so far.

IAN: (*Slightly sharply*) Dafydd?

GUY: Yes. I presume he's acting for you on this.

IAN: Yes, yes. Maybe he is. (*Slight pause.*) Don't take this the
wrong way but – I could make this worth your while . . . I
think I can speak for Fay and say we both could . . . (*He
looks up at the picture and winks.*) OK?
(*The doorbell rings.*)
Ah, that'll be your friend. (*Yelling*) Doorbell, doll . . . (*To*
GUY) The sort that likes to keep you waiting, is she? (*He
grins.*)

56

GUY: Well, not if she can help it. She may have fallen over, of
    course . . .
IAN: Fallen over? What is she? On skates?
    (FAY *enters. She carries the drinks.*)
    Where is she then?
FAY: You have to answer it.
IAN: Why?
FAY: Because you have to . . .
IAN: Oh, all right. (*He moves to the door.*)
FAY: (*Giving him a drink*) Here.
IAN: (*Taking it*) Ta.
    (IAN *goes out.*)
FAY: (*Calling after him.*) You may need it. (*To* GUY) Quick,
    quick . . . (*Dragging him to the window*) Here. Have a look.
    Is that your friend? My God, it must be. (*She giggles.*)
GUY: Yes. That's Dilys. She looks a bit the worse for wear.
    Hope she's all right . . .
FAY: Come on. Quick . . . (*She drags him again, this time to the
    door.*) Bring your drink . . .
GUY: Why, where . . . ?
FAY: Beddy-bys . . .
GUY: Sorry?
FAY: I'm in desperate need of veal. Now.
GUY: (*As she drags him off*) Veal? What, in bed . . .
    (*As they leave,* IAN's *voice is heard returning along the hall.*)
IAN: (*Off*) Yes, well, perhaps you'd like to tidy up in the
    bathroom. (*Entering, speaking back to someone behind him*)
    The light's just inside the door. Can you manage? That's it
    . . . Well done . . .
    (*He stands in the doorway with his drink.*)
    (*Stunned*) Bloody hellfire. (*He drains his glass.*)
    (*The lights fade on him and come up on a section of moonlit
    street.* GUY, *paralytically drunk, staggers into view. He stops
    under a street lamp.*)
GUY: (*Bellowing into the night*) Fear not, good citizens, now
    abed. Matt of the Mint is here. The highwayman with the
    hole in the middle. Matt of the Mint. V.E.A.L. Voraciously
    Enterprising Acrobatic Lover . . .

(GUY *starts to sing. Drunkenly unaccompanied at first and then, as the scene changes, as part of the rehearsal, along with the other three men,* MR AMES *accompanying.* DAFYDD *paces about watching.*)

(*Singing, as Matt*) Let us take the Road.
Hark! I hear the sound of Coaches!
The hour of Attack approaches,
To your Arms, brave Boys, and load,
See the Ball I hold!
Let the Chemists toil like Asses,
Our Fire their Fire surpasses,
And turns all our Lead to Gold.
Hoorah! Hoorah! Hoorah!

(*The song ends triumphantly.* TED, CRISPIN, JARVIS *and* GUY *clink their papier mâché tankards with great dash.* BRIDGET *is back on the book.*)

DAFYDD: Excellent. Bravo. Well done all, thank you. Couple of minutes and we're going on to Macheath and the ladies. Guy, please, could I have a moment?

(TED, CRISPIN *and* JARVIS *are making their way backstage.*)
No, no, Crispin, don't go away, boy. I need you in a minute.

(CRISPIN *remains behind.* TED *and* JARVIS *go off.*)
(*To* GUY) He's like an animal, that boy. Only got to mention a coffee break and he's got his trousers round his knees. He's got both those girls on a string, you know. Linda and Bridget. It's not fair on the rest of us, is it . . . ?

(*He laughs.*
GUY *manages a smile.*)
Now. Just a word, Guy. Fay's just had a chat with me. And. Well, it's Ian. According to Fay, he doesn't think he's going to be able to do the part after all. So. We are now without a Filch. Which is serious, because it's a very big part indeed. So. I think you know what's coming, Guy. What do you say? Filch. Could you do it?

(*The women, mustered by* BRIDGET, *are beginning to assemble on the other side of the stage. They are* REBECCA, FAY, HANNAH, ENID *and* LINDA.)

GUY: Well . . .

DAFYDD: You know, a month ago I wouldn't even have considered asking you but – lately . . . It's doing you good, these dramatics. You're growing in confidence every day. Can I take it you'll agree?

GUY: All right.

DAFYDD: Good man. (*He shakes* GUY's *hand.*)

GUY: And . . . thank you.

DAFYDD: Don't thank me. Thank Fay. She suggested you straightaway. Of course, I agreed. (*Moving to address the assembly as a whole*) Ladies and gentlemen, I'd like to run the dance, please . . . Take your places. But just before we do, unfortunately I have to announce yet another cast change. Unavoidably, Ian Hubbard has had to withdraw from his featured role as Filch and that part will now be taken by our all-purpose replacement, Mr Guy Jones. (*All the women applaud.*)

REBECCA: I said he should have played it in the first place.

DAFYDD: There is, however, no truth in the rumour that, at his present rate of progress, he will shortly be taking over from yours truly. (*He laughs. One or two looks are exchanged.*) Thank you, Mr Ames. (*A dance. The women parade around* CRISPIN *as Macheath.*)

WOMEN: (*Singing*) Youth's the Season made for Joys,

CRISPIN: (*Singing, as Macheath*) Love is then our Duty,

WOMEN: She alone who that employs,

CRISPIN: (*As Macheath*) Well deserves her Beauty.

WOMEN: Let's be gay,

While we may,

Beauty's a Flower, despised in decay.

Youth's the Season (*etc.*)

Let us drink and sport to-day

CRISPIN: (*As Macheath*) Ours is not tomorrow.

WOMEN: Love with Youth flies swift away,

CRISPIN: (*As Macheath*) Age is nought but sorrow

WOMEN: Dance and sing,

Time's on the Wing,

Life never knows the return of Spring.
Let us drink (*etc.*)

DAFYDD: (*Calling encouragement*) Come on, Ladies, give it some body, some body . . . remember these are all pimps and whores. Horizontal women. All of them . . .

REBECCA: (*Softly but audibly*) Some of us may be . . .

DAFYDD: Come on, Linda, head up, try and sell it to us. Sell us your body, Linda . . .

BRIDGET: (*With a laugh*) She couldn't give it away . . .

DAFYDD: Bridget, shut up . . . (*To the dancers*) That's it . . . good . . . better . . .
(*As the dance is finishing*) And we all look towards Macheath and curtsy . . .
(*The women are all turned in* GUY's *direction except for* ENID *who, quite correctly, is facing* CRISPIN. *Seeing she is the only one doing this she hastens to conform with the others.*)
(*Seizing* ENID *and shaking her furiously*) No, not at him, at Macheath. Macheath . . . Oh, I give up . . .
(*The music ends.* CRISPIN *goes.*)
All right. Thank you very much everyone. Fifteen minutes. Thank you.
(DAFYDD, MR AMES *and* BRIDGET *leave. The women follow, discussing as they go the events of the dance and in particular sympathizing, some of them anyway, with the luckless* ENID.)

BRIDGET: (*As they go*) The kettle's on . . .
(GUY *is left alone for a moment. He rises to follow the rest of them. He seems to us very pleased with life thus far.*)

ACT TWO

*The overall scene is very much the same; the time, a little later on
into rehearsals. At the start, a light comes up on* CRISPIN *as
Macheath.*

CRISPIN: (*sings, as Macheath*)
    If the Heart of a Man is deprest with Cares;
    The Mist is dispell'd when a Woman appears;
    Like the Notes of a Fiddle, she sweetly, sweetly
    Raises the Spirits and charms our Ears.
    Roses and Lillies her Cheeks disclose,
    But her ripe Lips are more sweet than those.
    Press her, caress her, with Blisses her Kisses
    Dissolve us in Pleasure, and soft Repose.
    (*As the song finishes, we crossfade to a café table. Basically a
    'four', at present it contains just* GUY *and* HANNAH. *Used cups
    and plates and a cakestand with several cakes still remaining.*
    HANNAH *is eating one of these. There is a tense air about the
    scene. Most of the tension, it would appear, being generated by*
    HANNAH.)
HANNAH: (*After a pause*) Well. What are you going to do about
    it? (*Pause.*) I mean, you can't have both of us, can you?
    (*Pause.*) You can't have your . . . (*She tails off as she looks
    at the cakestand.*) You'll just have to make up your mind,
    Guy. Me or her.
GUY: (*Muttering unhappily*) It's not – that – easy . . .
HANNAH: What? What did you say?
GUY: (*Rather too loudly*) I said it's not that easy . . .
HANNAH: Sshh! Sshh! All right. Do you want the whole
    restaurant to hear us? (*Pause.*) I mean, why do you want
    two of us, anyway?
GUY: I don't want two of you –
HANNAH: Isn't one enough?
GUY: I love you both in – different ways . . .
HANNAH: I'm glad to hear it. I suppose I'm the one who's good

61

for sewing on buttons and doing your washing. That takes a great deal of arranging, I'll have you know. Using our machine while Dafydd's out of the way. Sorting out socks at midnight. (*A sudden practical thought.*) You don't have any of his pants, do you? He's mislaid a pair.

GUY: Sort of Paisley patterned?

HANNAH: Those are them. If you have them, give me them back, will you?

GUY: I think I've got them on, actually.

HANNAH: Oh, God. Guy.

(*Pause.*)

Well, it's obvious you don't go to Fay for your washing. Despite all those pale clothes she wears, I always get the feeling that there's something very grubby underneath.

GUY: Oh, come on, Hannah. (*Pause.*) Have a cake.

HANNAH: I've had quite enough cake. And I'm sick to death of us meeting in cafés and pubs and bus shelters . . .

GUY: Well, where else can we go?

HANNAH: Nowhere. It's too small a town. Everybody knows.

GUY: Yes, I know.

HANNAH: Except Dafydd, of course.

GUY: No. I honestly don't think he does know. I thought at first he was turning a gigantic blind eye but . . .

HANNAH: Dafydd doesn't know. He's amazing. Even the twins are suspicious. They've started calling that Daddy-doll of theirs Guy. Fortunately, Dafydd just thinks they're starting early for bonfire night. (*Pause.*) No, he doesn't want me – in that way – any more, so he assumes no one else could possibly – want me. (*Pause.*) I'm not sure anyone does, really.

(*She cries. Angry tears.*)

GUY: Hannah. Now, Hannah . . .

HANNAH: (*Savagely*) It's just damn lucky for you that Dafydd doesn't know about us, that's all I can say. Otherwise he'd sort you out, he really would. He'd beat you senseless. He'd punch you into a pulp. He'd smash your face in and jump on you and he'd kick you where it really hurt. And I'd laugh. Ha! Ha!

He's bloody tough. He was a rugger player, you know . . .

GUY: Yes. Yes, he told me.

(HANNAH *sobs*.)

Please don't, Hannah. Please . . . People are staring. I'll get the bill.

HANNAH: (*Seeing someone behind* GUY) Oh, no . . .

GUY: What is it?

HANNAH: It's her. She followed us here. She's spying on us.

GUY: Oh, Lord . . .

(FAY *comes into view. She has evidently been shopping. She carries several bags.*)

FAY: Hallo, you two.

(HANNAH *ignores her.*)

GUY: Hallo, Fay.

FAY: What a funny place to come for tea. A right little clip joint . . .

HANNAH: Is that why you're here?

FAY: (*Sitting at the table between them*) May I join you?

HANNAH: You most certainly may not.

FAY: Thank you. Whew! I'm exhausted. You look terrible, Hannah. What is it, darling, hay fever?

HANNAH: I'm allergic, that's all. To certain smells.

(FAY *regards* HANNAH *for a moment. A silence.*)

GUY: Look, this is all very awkward. I think it would be better if one of us left, I really do.

FAY: It's all right. I'm not stopping . . .

HANNAH: Good.

FAY: I just wanted to give something to Guy.

HANNAH: What?

(FAY *produces a paper bag from amongst her shopping.*)

FAY: (*Passing it to* GUY) Here . . .

HANNAH: What is it?

FAY: Private.

HANNAH: (*Taking hold of the bag*) What?

FAY: Mind your own business . . .

HANNAH: I demand to know what it is. I demand to know . . .

FAY: Get your hands off . . .

GUY: (*Interceding, mildly*) Now, now. Now then. Come on, girls, people are . . . (*He smiles round the restaurant.*)
(HANNAH *and* FAY *stay deadlocked.*)

FAY: Then tell her to let go.

HANNAH: I refuse to allow her to walk in here and start giving you things . . .

GUY: Hannah . . .

HANNAH: How dare she give you secret presents right under my nose . . . She's just trying to humiliate me. That's what she's doing . . .

FAY: Let go.

HANNAH: No.

GUY: Look. Let's be adult about this, shall we? (*Looking at them in turn*) Girls? Please. Look, let me have it. And I'll open it. And then there'll be no secrets. All right? Hannah? Hannah . . .

HANNAH: All right. I want to see.

GUY: Fay?

FAY: (*Shrugging*) Fine with me . . .
(*They release the bag to* GUY.)

GUY: Right. OK. Now then. (*Opening the bag and removing the contents*) Let's see what we have in . . .
(*He holds a pair of Paisley-patterned pants.*)
Oh, God.

FAY: They were under the bed. I didn't want you to catch cold. (*She giggles.*)

HANNAH: (*Looking at* FAY *with extreme loathing*) You total bitch. You total and utter grubby, smutty, grimy, unhygienic little bitch. (*Snatching at the pants*) Give me those. Give me those at once . . .

GUY: (*Holding them still*) Hannah . . .

FAY: Don't do that . . .

HANNAH: Give them to me . . .

FAY: (*Joining in the tussle*) Let go, at once . . .

GUY: Now this is silly. Now come on . . .
(*They tug.*)

HANNAH: Give me those pants . . .

FAY: Hannah, they are not yours. Now let go. They don't belong to you . . .

HANNAH: Oh, yes they do . . .

FAY: Nonsense . . .

GUY: I think they do actually, Fay.

FAY: They're hers?

HANNAH: Yes.

FAY: (*Letting go*) Darling. I'm terribly sorry . . .

GUY: (*Also letting go*) I mean, when I say hers I meant –

FAY: Hannah, darling, who ever would have guessed? It just goes to show. Behind the most boring exterior . . .

HANNAH: (*Stuffing the pants into her handbag*) How dare you do this? How dare you . . . ?

FAY: . . . lurk the weirdest of hang-ups . . .

GUY: Fay, please . . .

HANNAH: (*Rising and putting on her coat*) I'm not stopping here . . .

FAY: Don't worry, darling, your secret is safe.

HANNAH: (*To* FAY) You'll be sorry for this. I promise you, you'll be sorry for this . . .
(HANNAH *goes out.*)

GUY: (*Rising*) Oh, Fay . . . Really. There was no need for that. Really.

FAY: Oh. Are you going?

GUY: Yes, of course. I've got to . . . (*He indicates* HANNAH.)

FAY: Help her choose a jock strap . . .

GUY: Fay, please, don't keep on. Those are Dafydd's . . .

FAY: Dafydd's?

GUY: Of course they were . . .

FAY: Curiouser and curiouser . . .

GUY: A mix-up in the wash. That's all . . .

FAY: I shan't enquire further, darling. Don't worry. I'll see you this evening, then. At rehearsal.

GUY: Rather.

FAY: And I'll be in later, if you want to pop round . . .

GUY: (*Doubtfully*) Well . . . Not this evening, Fay . . .

FAY: By the way, Ian was asking if you'd heard anything yet. About the land.

GUY: Oh. No. Sorry.

FAY: Only Jarvis is not going to hang on for ever. If we don't
buy it somebody else will.

GUY: Jarvis? You mean it's Jarvis who owns it?

FAY: (*Feeling she may have said too much*) Yes. Didn't you know?
I thought you did.

GUY: No, I didn't realize he owned it.

FAY: (*Shrugging*) Not that it matters. The point is, have you
been asking? Because that was part of our deal, darling,
wasn't it?

GUY: Deal? How do you mean?

FAY: I mean, Ian did give up his role for you, didn't he? Filch.

GUY: Oh, Filch. Yes. I didn't ask him to, you know.

FAY: No, but you didn't say no, did you? But then you haven't
actually said no to anything, have you? Not that I'm
complaining. But I suppose Ian might. Eventually. If you
don't come up with the goods.

GUY: Well, I am . . . I am asking round. Discreetly, of course.

FAY: Oh, good. It'd be horrid if it all got nasty, wouldn't it?
Bye-bye, darling.

GUY: (*Rather uneasily*) Bye . . .

(GUY *goes rather unhappily.* FAY *sits on at her table for a
minute, smiling to herself. A light comes up on* LINDA.)

LINDA: (*As Lucy, sings*)

Thus when a good Huswife sees a Rat

In her Trap in the Morning taken,

With pleasure her Heart goes pit a pat,

In Revenge for her loss of Bacon.

Then she throws him

To the Dog or Cat,

To be worried, crushed and shaken.

(*As the song ends,* FAY *exits. General lights come up on* LINDA
to reveal she is in rehearsal with both HANNAH *and* CRISPIN,
as Polly and Macheath. Also in attendance, BRIDGET *with the
prompt script, as usual.* DAFYDD *is prowling the auditorium
and, away in one corner paying little attention,* JARVIS *sits with
a small portable cassette player clipped to his person and a pair
of lightweight headphones clamped to his ears. He is in a
private world of his own.* GUY, *who has entered during the song,*

66

also watches the ensuing rehearsal. CRISPIN *stands holding a freestanding mock-up rehearsal gaol door, through which he plays the scene.*)

LINDA: (*As Lucy, speaking*) Am I then bilk'd of my Virtue? Can I have no Reparation? Sure Men were born to lye, and Women to believe them! O Villain! Villain!

HANNAH: (*As Polly*) Am I not thy Wife? – Thy Neglect of me, thy Aversion to me too severely proves it. – Look on me. – Tell me, am I not thy Wife?

LINDA: (*As Lucy*) Perfidious Wretch!

HANNAH: (*As Polly*) Barbarous Husband!

LINDA: (*As Lucy*) Hadst thou been hang'd five Months ago, I had been happy.

HANNAH: (*As Polly*) And I too – if you had been kind to me 'till Death, it would not have vex'd me – And that's no very unreasonable Request, (though from a Wife) to a Man who hath not above seven or eight Days to live.
(*Under this last exchange,* DAFYDD *seeing* GUY *has joined the rehearsal strolls over to him.*)

DAFYDD: (*In a loud whisper*) Sorry. We're running a bit late. Be with you in a second.

GUY: (*Sotto*) OK.

DAFYDD: Bloody hard work it is with these three. This lad – great voice. But he moves like something out of Austin Reed's window. And as for this prissy little madam . . .
(*Indicates* LINDA.) Look at her. I've seen rougher trade on a health food counter . . .
(*The rehearsal continues.*)

LINDA: (*As Lucy*) Are thou then married Monster? . . . (*She hesitates.*)

BRIDGET: (*Prompting loudly*) Art thou then married to another?

LINDA: (*As Lucy*) Art thou then married to another? Hast thou –

BRIDGET: (*Interrupting her*) Has thou two Wives, Monster?

LINDA: All right, all right, I know it . . .

BRIDGET: I was giving you the line . . .

LINDA: Yes, well, I knew it. I knew it, didn't I?
(HANNAH *wanders away from the exchange. There's evidently*

been quite a lot of this sort of thing. CRISPIN *remains amusedly detached.* DAFYDD *returns his attention to the rehearsal.*)

DAFYDD: All right, all right, girls. Come on, get on with it now.

LINDA: Every time I pause for breath, she reads out my line. Would you kindly ask her not to, please?

DAFYDD: Bridget, don't read her lines out unless she asks for them. And Linda, you stop pausing for so much breath.

LINDA: I have to breathe, don't I?

BRIDGET: (*In an undertone*) Not necessarily . . .

DAFYDD: You can't take that long breathing onstage. You want to breathe deeply, you breathe offstage in your own time . . . on we go. And Bridget, shut up!

BRIDGET: (*Muttering to herself*) I thought the only reason I was here was to prompt. I mean, what's the point of sitting here for three months . . . ?

DAFYDD: Bridget. Shut up! Go on.

(*A slight pause. The women look at* CRISPIN.)

CRISPIN: Oh, it's my go, is it? Right. (*As Macheath*) If Women's Tongues can cease for an Answer – hear me.
(DAFYDD *whimpers audibly at* CRISPIN's *effort.*)
(*Looking out in* DAFYDD's *direction*) I heard that . . .

LINDA: (*As Lucy*) I won't. – Flesh and Blood can't bear my Usage.

HANNAH: (*As Polly*) Shall I not claim my own? Justice bids me speak. Sure, my Dear, there ought to be some Preference shown to a Wife! At least she may claim the Appearance of it. (*Pointedly in* GUY's *direction*) He must be distracted with his Misfortunes, or he could not use me thus!
(*Another silence.* HANNAH *looks at* LINDA.)

LINDA: (*Realizing belatedly that it's her*) Um. Oh. Yes. Um. Oh. Eee. (*She twists herself in knots trying to remember. To* BRIDGET, *reluctantly*) What is it, then?

BRIDGET: (*Prompting*) Oh . . .

LINDA: (*Repeating her*) Oh . . .

BRIDGET: (*Forming the first syllable of 'villain'*) V . . . v . . .

LINDA: (*With her*) V . . . v . . . vain . . . vish . . . voo . . . ver . . . ver . . .

DAFYDD: (*Screaming from the back*) Look, what the hell is this, twenty bloody questions?

LINDA: (*Wailing*) She won't tell me my line . . .

DAFYDD: Bridget, for God's sake, tell her her line . . .

BRIDGET: You just told me not to. (*Reading rapidly*) Oh villain villain thou hast deceiv'd me I could even inform against thee with pleasure not a prude wishes more heartily to have facts against her intimate acquaintance . . .

(LINDA *starts wailing during this monotone rendition by* BRIDGET.)

DAFYDD: Bridget! That'll do . . .

(BRIDGET *stops*.)

BRIDGET: (*Innocently*) What?

HANNAH: (*Comforting* LINDA) Now, come on, dear . . .

LINDA: (*Scarcely audible, weeping*) She does that all the time. She keeps doing it. All the time . . .

(DAFYDD *gives a vast groan of impatience*.)

HANNAH: Just a minute, Dafydd, just a minute . . .

(*A very private women's huddle between* LINDA *and* HANNAH *that none of us can hear*. CRISPIN, *the root cause of all this, stands looking quite pleased with himself. He pulls faces at* DAFYDD *through the gaol door*.)

DAFYDD: (*To* GUY) Look at that smirking oaf. I wish to God they were professionals. Then I could sack them. These bastards, they've got you over a barrel. Unless you say well done all the time they don't turn up. What are those two doing? It's like a loose scrum. (*Yelling*) Come on, injury time's over. Give her a slice of lemon, change her shorts, and get her back on the field.

HANNAH: (*Leaving* LINDA, *to* DAFYDD) Right. She's all right. (*To* LINDA) All right?

(LINDA *nods and resumes her position*.)

LINDA: (*As Lucy, in a colourless tone, growing increasingly inaudible*) O Villain, Villain! (*She sniffs*.) Thou has deceiv'd me – (*Sniffs*.) I could even inform against thee with Pleasure. Not a Prude wishes more heartily to have Facts against her intimate Acquaintance, than I now wish to have Facts against thee. I would have her Satisfaction, and they should all out . . . (*She peters out*.)

DAFYDD: (*Who has moved closer and closer to her in an attempt to hear*) And . . . Mr Ames! Don't tell me he's died now. Mr Ames . . .

MR AMES: (*Cheerily*) Hallo?

DAFYDD: Song.

MR AMES: Sorry. (*He starts to play.*)

HANNAH: (*Singing, as Polly*) I'm bubbled.

LINDA: (*Singing, as Lucy*) I'm bubbled.

HANNAH: Oh how I am troubled!

LINDA: Bamboozled and bit!

HANNAH: My Distresses are doubled.

LINDA: When you come to the Tree, should the Hangman refuse,

These fingers, with Pleasure, could fasten the Noose.

HANNAH: I'm bubbled, (*etc.*)

(*The song ends. The scene resumes without pause.*)

(*Speaking, as Polly*) And hast thou the Heart to persist in disowning me?

CRISPIN: (*As Macheath*) And hast thou the Heart to persist in persuading me that I am married? Why, Polly, dost thou seek to aggravate my Misfortunes?

(DAFYDD *groans again at this rendition.*)

LINDA: (*As Lucy*) Really, Miss Peachum, you but expose yourself.

(BRIDGET *sniggers.*)

Besides . . . (*Crossing to* BRIDGET, *furiously*) Will you stop laughing at me? Will you stop laughing?

DAFYDD: (*From the back*) Hey, hey, hey, hey . . .

BRIDGET: It was funny . . .

HANNAH: Linda . . .

LINDA: I'll soon make you stop laughing.

(*She grabs the unprepared* BRIDGET *by her hair and hauls her off her chair and on to the floor.*)

BRIDGET: (*Furious*) OW . . .

CRISPIN: (*With great relish*) Wey-hey!

LINDA: I'll teach you, I'll teach you . . .

BRIDGET: Now, let go. Let go, I'm warning you . . .

HANNAH: Oh, dear heavens. That's it. That's it. No more . . .

DAFYDD: (*Ineffectually, trying to part them*) Now come on, girls, come on . . .

(JARVIS's *attention has been attracted by the scrap onstage.*)

JARVIS: (*To* DAFYDD, *loudly because of his headphones*) Good scrap that. Very convincing. First class.

DAFYDD: Oh, shut up.

(JARVIS *does not hear but smiles. The girls are fighting in earnest now. Close combat stuff, on the floor, rolling over and over, both seeking for an advantage.* BRIDGET's *greater strength is matched by* LINDA's *white fury.* MR AMES, *at* CRISPIN's *beckoning, starts up another song. During the course of this, the fight continues silently until* GUY *and* DAFYDD *manage to prise the girls apart. All this in mimed silence, although presumably in reality the din is quite loud.*)

CRISPIN: (*Singing, together with* MR AMES, *with unusual relish*)
How happy could I be with either,
Were t'other dear Charmer away!
But while you thus teaze me together,
To neither a Word will I say;
But tol de rol, (*etc.*)
(*As the song finishes, 'normal sound' is resumed. The combatants are panting and exhausted. So are the rescuers.* GUY *is holding* BRIDGET; HANNAH *holds* LINDA. DAFYDD *stands between them, gasping to regain his breath, before speaking.* JARVIS *has watched it all from his ringside seat with great enjoyment.*)

DAFYDD: (*At length*) All right now . . . listen to me . . . both of you . . .
(BRIDGET *attempts to struggle free from* GUY. GUY *clings on.*)
Now come along, Bridget. Bridget! Bridget . . .
(DAFYDD *makes to slap* BRIDGET's *face. She quietens. He goes to pat her instead. She snaps at his hand and he all but loses his fingers.*)
Jesus! All right . . .
(LINDA *starts to struggle, too.*)

HANNAH: I can't hold her much . . .

DAFYDD: (*To* HANNAH) All right, take her backstage. Backstage. Run her under a tap.

(HANNAH *starts to drag* LINDA *off*.)

(*To* GUY) And her. Outside. (*Assisting* GUY *with* BRIDGET)
All right, I've got her. Come on. Outside, you. Outside.
(HANNAH *takes* LINDA *off*. GUY *and* DAFYDD *take* BRIDGET
out, lifting her between them. DAFYDD *returns almost
immediately*. GUY *presumably remains outside in case*
BRIDGET *decides to return*. DAFYDD *now turns his attention to
the smirking* CRISPIN.)

DAFYDD: As for you, you sniggering Herbert. This is all your
fault. You were entirely to blame for that.

CRISPIN: Bollocks. (*He goes to leave*.)

DAFYDD: (*After him*) I've a good mind to sort you out, boy, I
really have.

CRISPIN: (*Turning suddenly, violently*) Right you are. You're on.

DAFYDD: (*Taken aback somewhat by this change of tone*) What?

CRISPIN: Come on, then . . .

DAFYDD: No, that's not the way. Violence is no solution.

CRISPIN: I've been longing to have a go at you. Come on.
(CRISPIN *starts to advance slightly on* DAFYDD. *He, in turn,
retreats rather apprehensively*.)
You've been getting up my nose for a few weeks now . . .

DAFYDD: Now come on, boy, be your age. Ah ah. Now, now.
I'm a . . . I'm a middle-aged man, you know. Very nearly.
That wouldn't be fair. Let's be reasonable . . . Now, don't
you . . . don't you try it . . . I'm a lawyer, you know . . . I
could have you for . . . I won't, of course, if you don't . . .
(*Nose to nose with* CRISPIN, *unable to retreat further,
nervously*) Well, now what? Eh? (*He laughs*.)

CRISPIN: Well . . .

DAFYDD: Yes?

CRISPIN: How about this for starters?
(CRISPIN *brings his knee up sharply and moves back*. DAFYDD
gives a fearful whistling sound and bends double. HANNAH *and*
GUY *have both returned separately to witness this*.)

HANNAH: Dafydd . . .

GUY: Hoy . . .

CRISPIN: (*Cheerfully*) Bye all . . . (*He strolls out*.)

DAFYDD: (*In pain*) Oooooorrrggg.

72

JARVIS: (*Who was watching this*) No, that wasn't as convincing as the other one . . .

DAFYDD: (*Glaring at* JARVIS, *his face twisted in malignant pain*) I'll kill him. I'll kill that old bastard . . .

JARVIS: (*Smiling, unhearing*) You don't mind an opinion, do you?

GUY: You OK?

HANNAH: Is he all right?

GUY: Yes, I think he's been hit in the . . .

HANNAH: (*Sympathetically*) Oh, yes. It's very painful there, isn't it?

DAFYDD: Of course it's bloody painful . . .

GUY: Cold water helps . . . I think.

HANNAH: Right. Well, you . . . (*Starting to lead* DAFYDD *away*) You'd better come and sit with Linda. You can have the sink after her . . .
(*They start going off,* HANNAH *picking up* LINDA'*s bag on their way.* DAFYDD *groans.*)
Carefully, dear. That's it . . .
(HANNAH *and* DAFYDD *go off.*)

GUY: (*To himself*) Oh, well . . .

JARVIS: (*Removing his headphones and offering them to* GUY) Have a listen to that. Tell me what you think it is.
(GUY *somewhat reluctantly puts on the headphones. Whatever he hears is very loud and not too pleasant. He hastily takes them off.*)

GUY: God! What is it?

JARVIS: Give up? That is an actual recording of an 1812 Boulton and Watt beam engine which is still used to this day for pumping water to the summit of the Kennet and Avon canal.

GUY: Good heavens.

JARVIS: It lifts one ton of water 40 feet on each stroke of the engine.

GUY: Amazing.

JARVIS: That's what I've been listening to for the past hour.

GUY: A beam engine?

JARVIS: Aye.

GUY: What, all evening?

JARVIS: No, no, no. This is called 'The Vanishing Sounds in

Britain'. Issued by the BBC. All vanishing sounds . . .

GUY: Well, listening to that, it's probably a good job, isn't it? (*He laughs.*)

JARVIS: (*Not hearing*) What's that? (*He switches off the recorder.*) No, I gave the record to the wife last Christmas, but she wasn't so keen . . .

GUY: Look. May I have a quick word with you? (*Looking round to see that they're alone*) It's about a piece of land that apparently belongs to you. Round the back of the BLM factory. Do you know it?

JARVIS: I not only know it. I own it.

GUY: Yes.

JARVIS: I'll tell you a very interesting little tale about that bit of land . . .

GUY: (*His heart sinking*) Oh, really . . .

JARVIS: That land was purchased by my grandfather, old Joshua Pike, for the benefit of his employees. He were a philanthropist and a deeply religious man – chapel, you see – but his other passion, apart from t'firm, were cricket. Cricket mad. You with me?

GUY: Aye. Yes.

JARVIS: Well, he bought that land off a widow woman and he had his lads, his workers, levelling and draining and returfing it – in their own time, mind – not his. And, well, when it were finished – well, some said it were the finest strip for a hundred mile or more. Like a billiard pool. And he said to the lads, there you are, lads, go to it. That's my gift to you. That's my bounty.

GUY: Wonderful.

JARVIS: Only one thing – bearing in mind he were a chapel man – not on Sundays, lads. Never on the sabbath. Well, any road up, year or so later, he's out for a stroll one Sunday afternoon with his children and his grandchildren – taking the air, like – and what should he spy as he's passing the cricket field but a bunch of workers laughing and joking and chucking a ball about like it were Saturday dinner time. And the old man says nowt. Not at the time. But the next day, Monday morning first thing, he sends in his bulldozers

74

and diggers and ploughs and he digs that land up from one end to the other. Then he sets fire to t'pavilion and he puts up a 12-foot wooden fence. Palings. And to this day, not a ball has been thrown on that field. That's the sort of man he was. Me grandfather. Dying breed.

GUY: Another vanishing sound of Britain. Yes . . . (*After what he hopes is a respectful pause*) The point is, with regard to this land . . . There is a rumour, unconfirmed I may add, that BLM are contemplating buying it. Possibly. In which case it could be worth a bit. If you were considering selling it.

(JARVIS *considers this.*)

So.

JARVIS: Say no more.

GUY: You follow me.

JARVIS: I'm glad of the information. I trust you. You're a Scotty. And I'll see you're looked after, don't worry.

GUY: No, I don't need looking after. Really.

JARVIS: Then why are you telling me?

GUY: Well, I – thought you ought to know – it's just that I wouldn't want people to put one over on you. Friendly.

JARVIS: (*Laughing sceptically*) Friendly? Oh, aye? That's a good one.

GUY: Well, if you don't believe me . . .

JARVIS: Don't come the friendly with me, friend. I've a few years to go yet but when I leave this earth, I'll be leaving it fair and square. Same as me father did and me grandfather. I owe nothing to no one. They're all paid off. I've paid off my business. I've paid off my family. There's no claim on me from any quarter. And I don't intend to start making exceptions with you. You see me right. I'll see you right. Right?

GUY: Right.

(REBECCA *comes in from the road. She is in time to catch the end of this conversation. She looks at them a trifle suspiciously.*)

REBECCA: Hello.

JARVIS: Aye.

GUY: Good evening.

REBECCA: Has Dafydd got to us yet?

GUY: No. I don't think he's got to very much, actually . . .

REBECCA: How unsurprising. Where is he? Back there?

GUY: Yes.

REBECCA: I'll sort them out then. I've had enough of this . . .

(REBECCA *goes backstage*.)

JARVIS: I've paid her off and all. My mother's 92. She's paid off.

GUY: You paid your mother off?

JARVIS: A hundred quid a week tax free and a bungalow in Paignton. She's not complaining. (*As he moves to go backstage*) You'll be paid off. Don't worry . . .

(JARVIS *goes off*. GUY, *alone and as keen as ever, decides to have a quick private rehearsal. He takes up his script. He reads other people's lines but tries to speak his own without looking*.)

GUY: (*Reading*) Come hither Filch . . . blurr, blurr, blurr . . . (*He skips*.) Where was your Post last Night, my Boy? (*Without the script*) I ply'd at the Opera, Madam; and considering 'twas neither dark nor rainy, so that there was no great Hurry in getting Chairs and Coaches, Made a tolerable on't. These seven Handkerchiefs, Madam.

(GUY *checks the script and is pleased to see he got it right. He is about to continue when he sees* DAFYDD *has appeared. He is very subdued and is sipping a beaker of tea*.)

How are you feeling?

DAFYDD: Oh, pretty good. Like a man who's just spent his wedding night with an electrified steam shovel . . .

(GUY *nods sympathetically*.)

Well. Now we are in a hole. If that boy doesn't come back we're over the dead-ball line, I can tell you. Trying to do *The Beggar's Opera* without a Macheath is a bit of a non-starter even for Peter Brook. So. (*Pause*.) Oh, it makes you want to . . . Who cares, anyway? Who cares?

GUY: I do.

DAFYDD: Ah, Guy, Guy. My rock. But nobody really cares. Not in this country. Anything you want to mention's more important than theatre to most of them. Washing their hair, cleaning their cars . . . If this was Bulgaria or somewhere we'd have peasants hammering on the doors. Demanding satisfaction or their money back. This place, you tell them you're interested in the arts, you get messages of sympathy. Get well soon. Well, maybe they're right. Why beat your brains out? Every time I vow I'm just going to have a ball. I'm not going to take any of it seriously. It's just a play, for God's sake . . . And every time it gets like this. Desperate. Life and death stuff. Look at me. You'd think to look at me I was in really serious trouble. While all that's happened, in fact, is that a play might not happen. That's all. But of course the irony is that outside these four walls, in the real world out there, I actually am in serious trouble and I couldn't give a stuff. Now that really does raise questions, doesn't it? If I were my psychiatrist I'd be worried that all was not well. And I'd be right.

GUY: (*Cautiously*) Any – particular sort of trouble?

DAFYDD: (*Evasively*) Well, apart from being beaten up by a singing Yahoo . . . nothing very original. I don't know. Things, you know. Hannah. Things like that. (*Pause.*) She's a bloody deep-freeze of a woman. That's the trouble. Physically. I mean, she's great in other ways. Wonderful at keeping the home going and things. I mean without her . . . (*He smiles.*) I call her my Swiss Army Wife, you know. No man should be without one. (*He laughs.*) Yes, yes . . . It's just that she's – she's got a blade missing, if you know what I mean. Always has had. Isn't her fault of course. Just not in her nature. Right from our wedding night. Ice tongs to lift her nightdress, I'm telling you . . .

GUY: You didn't . . . find out – before you were married?

DAFYDD: Well, not from my part of Wales, boy. Not too hot on sale or return there, you know. Mind you, I assumed she'd thaw. Given a little warmth. And, you know, general encouragement. (*With more passion, suddenly*) God, it's not that I didn't try . . . I really wanted to make it work, I really did. The nights I spent – battering at those damn defences of hers. But nothing. Knock one down she'd build another.

GUY: (*Trying to lighten it*) Well. You managed to have twins . . .

DAFYDD: (*Darkly*) Yes. Well, we never talk about that. Never.

GUY: Ah . . .

DAFYDD: Sorry, Guy. Bloody bore. I'm sorry. Why should I bore you with me and Hannah? Sorry . . . Don't know what came over me. I think it takes a kick in the crutch to make a man painfully aware of his own mortality . . .

(REBECCA *returns.*)

(*Irritably*) Yes?

REBECCA: Sorry to interrupt. First, I thought you'd like to know that the tannoy's on . . .

DAFYDD: Oh, God . . .

REBECCA: And second, in a vain attempt to prevent Hannah from hearing, we had a meeting . . .

DAFYDD: Oh, yes. And?

REBECCA: Well, what are we going to do? Scrap the production? I mean that boy, from all accounts, doesn't intend to come back, does he? So what do we do?

DAFYDD: I don't know what we do. You tell me. You're the one who keeps holding bloody meetings. Next time try inviting me. Maybe I can make a few suggestions.

REBECCA: Very well, to start with. We need a new Macheath. Agreed?

DAFYDD: Yes. And where are we going to find him? Eh?

REBECCA: Well . . . (*She looks towards* GUY.)

GUY: Ah.

DAFYDD: You mean Guy?

REBECCA: He's the natural choice, isn't he? It's either him or Ian Hubbard . . .

DAFYDD: Oh God, anyone rather than Ian Hubbard . . .

REBECCA: (*Pointing towards the tannoy mike*) Shh!

DAFYDD: Sorry. (*In a whisper*) Could you do it?

GUY: I –

REBECCA: Do it? He'd love it . . .

(*The lights close down to a single spot on* GUY. REBECCA *and* DAFYDD *leave.*)

GUY: (*Singing, as Macheath*)
Which way shall I turn me – How can I decide!

Wives, the Day of our Death, are as fond as a Bride.
One Wife is too much for most Husbands to hear,
But two at a time there's no Mortal can bear.
This way, and that way, and which way I will,
What would comfort the one, t'other wife would take ill.
(*At the end of the song, the lights come up on* REBECCA's
garden. A seat. A garden table. GUY *stands looking round.*)

REBECCA: (*Hailing him*) Yoo-hoo! Over here, Guy. It's so sweet
of you to pop round. Excuse the midges, won't you? Would
you like a cup of tea? Shall I ring for some tea?

GUY: No. No, thank you. Had my tea at home, just now.

REBECCA: Sure? A sherry or something?

GUY: No. Thanks all the same. Not with rehearsals in a
minute.

REBECCA: (*Picking up her own glass*) Quite right, quite right.
You put the rest of us to shame, Guy. Mind you, I don't
think it would matter that much if I drank myself silly.
They always manage to hide me behind a piece of scenery
anyway . . .
(*She laughs.* GUY *laughs politely.*)
Do sit down. (*Proffering a cigarette box*) Do you? No. You
are good. None of the vices. Practically. (*She smiles.*) We
all think you're going to be an absolutely wonderful
Macheath.

GUY: Thank you.

REBECCA: I take the view that Dafydd's terribly lucky to get
you. Whatever the price.

GUY: I'm sorry?

REBECCA: There's no need to be sorry. You've jollied us up no
end, Guy. All of us. In our different ways.

GUY: Well . . .

REBECCA: Now, what I'm really hoping is that you're going to
make my day as well. After all, you've made nearly
everybody else's. One way or another. It must be my turn,
mustn't it? Surely?
(REBECCA *smiles at him warmly.* GUY *shifts a little
uncomfortably. They are left thus as a light comes up on* TED,
ENID *and* JARVIS.)

TED, ENID *and* JARVIS: (*Singing*)
    In the days of my Youth I could bill like a Dove,
    Fa, la, la, (*etc.*)
    Like a sparrow at all times was ready for Love,
    Fa, la, la, (*etc.*)
    The Life of all Mortals in Kissing should pass,
    Lip to Lip while we're young – then the Lip to the Glass,
    Fa, la, la, (*etc.*)
    (*At the end of the song the lights return to their previous state.*
    REBECCA *and* GUY *have been chattering away.*)
REBECCA: Now. This little favour I wanted to ask . . . (*Seeing*
    GUY's *expression*) Don't look so terrified. It's not what
    you're thinking . . .
GUY: No, no. I was –
REBECCA: God forbid. Six years sharing a mattress with Jarvis
    cured me of that. No, it's just that I understand you and he
    were talking the other evening . . .
GUY: Yes? Oh, yes. About the –
REBECCA: About our little bit of land.
GUY: Yes. As a matter of fact I wanted to talk about that too,
    actually . . .
REBECCA: Good.
GUY: (*Fumbling in his pocket*) The point is I've – well, it's rather
    awkward – (*He produces a bulging envelope.*) I got this in the
    post this morning.
REBECCA: Oh, how gorgeous. (*Peering*) What is it? I'm sorry, I
    haven't my glasses.
GUY: It's £500.
REBECCA: Oh, super.
GUY: In notes. Cash.
REBECCA: Lucky you. What happened? Someone passed away?
GUY: Not – so far as I know. No. I rather thought it came from
    you.
REBECCA: Me?
GUY: Well, rather from Jarvis.
REBECCA: Jarvis?
GUY: I think so.
REBECCA: It sounds very unlikely. You'd be the first person who

managed to get money out of Jarvis. None of his wives ever could, I can tell you . . . Two of them died trying, poor things.

GUY: I'm pretty certain it is from him.

REBECCA: What does it say? With love from Jarvis?

GUY: Of course not. It's –

REBECCA: Then how do you know? Why on earth would my husband send you £500?

GUY: Because I – I warned him about this rumour. About the land. I can't at present find any foundation in truth in it, but there's this rumour that –

REBECCA: (*Slightly impatiently*) Yes, I've heard the rumour.

GUY: You have?

REBECCA: Oh, yes.

GUY: Well. I told Jarvis simply because I was anxious that he shouldn't be taken advantage of. Or you.

REBECCA: Well, that's awfully sweet of you. Thank you. Of course, it could work both ways, couldn't it? I mean, supposing this rumour wasn't true but everyone assumed it was, then the price would go up and Jarvis would be laughing. And the joke would be on these very unscrupulous people that you've so kindly been warning us about. Which would be a sort of poetic justice, wouldn't it?

GUY: Ah.

REBECCA: Of course, the whole thing would be helped tremendously if someone strategically placed like yourself did nothing to deny the rumour. Even, dare one say it, encouraged it?

GUY: Oh, I don't think I could . . .

REBECCA: No, no, heaven forbid. That's entirely up to your conscience. Anyway, you've got much too much on your mind already with Macheath. We mustn't worry you. Just remember, though, when they're all clapping and cheering you on the first night, it was me who got you the part. Remember that . . .

GUY: Yes. And I'm very grateful. I –

REBECCA: (*With the barest glance at her watch*) Now, we must dash, mustn't we? We don't want to keep them waiting. Do you have your car? (*She is moving away as she speaks.*)

GUY: Yes, thank you . . . You know, I'd really love to know how this rumour started. It's extraordinary . . .

REBECCA: (*Looking at him for a second and then realizing the question was without guile*) Well, I suspect that's something we shall never know, shall we? Any of us. Coming?

GUY: (*Indicating the envelope on the table*) What about – ? What shall I do with this? The money?

REBECCA: That's up to you, surely. Have fun with it, I should.

GUY: I can't accept it. Possibly.

REBECCA: Don't be so absurd.

GUY: No. If I took it, that would be . . . it'd be . . .

REBECCA: Well, suit yourself what you do with it. Only for heaven's sake don't leave it there. Or people might get the idea you were giving it to us. And that wouldn't look good at all, would it?

(REBECCA *goes out.* GUY *stares at the envelope undecided. He half moves away. He stops. After a second or so he returns to the money. He takes it up and pockets it. As he does so, the lights change and we are back in the rehearsal room.* GUY *now changes into his basic Macheath costume. He is assisted in this by several of the women in the company who fuss round him. Amongst these are* HANNAH, FAY, ENID *and* LINDA. *All of these are in part, most, or all of their costume. The production is entering its final phase. From here on we are very conscious that the production is 'lit'. While this activity ensues, silently,* BRIDGET, *also in costume for her role as Jenny Diver, sings:*)

BRIDGET: (*Sings, as Jenny*)

Before the Barn-door crowing,
The Cock by Hens attended,
His Eyes around him throwing,
Stands for a while suspended,
Then One he singles from the Crew,
And cheers the happy Hen;
With how do you do, and how do you do,
And how do you do again.

(*The other women sing with her at the chorus. As the song finishes, the lighting rehearsal continues.* GUY *remains midstage. The women and* MR AMES *leave the stage. The rehearsal has*

82

apparently been delayed for technical reasons. DAFYDD *enters from the lighting box.*)

DAFYDD: Sorry, Guy. We'll be underway pretty soon now. If nothing else blows up on us. (*Indicating the lighting box, confidentially*) He's slow, this electrician, though. Twenty minutes changing a colour. Unbelievable. I mean, why volunteer to light a show if you suffer from vertigo? He knew there'd be ladders. Man's a half-wit, he should . . . (*Another single light comes up on stage.*)
(*Calling to the box*) Thank you, Raymond, that's – that's lovely. (*Standing in a vivid orange patch of light, to* GUY) This look like firelight to you?

GUY: (*Uncertainly*) No. Not a lot.

DAFYDD: No, nor me. I'll cut it later. Better leave it for now. It took him three hours to focus . . . (*Calling again*) Yes, we're wild about that, Raymond. We like it very much. (*Consulting his plan*) Could I see your number 18 now, please? That's my number 15, your number 18. Thank you. (*To* GUY) Haven't even got the same bloody numbers, these plans . . . (*As a light comes up*) No, that's number 17, Raymond. That's your number 17. My number 12. The one I want to see is my number 15, your number 18.

RAYMOND: (*A distant voice.*) That is number 18 . . .

DAFYDD: What's that? No, that's number 17. My number 12. I don't want number 17. I want number 18. My number 18, your number 15.

RAYMOND: I haven't got a number 15 . . .

DAFYDD: No, hang on, as you were. *My* number 15. *Your* number 18 . . . (*Another lamp comes on.*) No, no, that's number 56. That shouldn't even be bloody plugged up . . . Hang on, hang on. For God's sake. I'm coming up, Raymond. And somebody, please open some doors. It's sub-tropical in here . . .
(DAFYDD *goes up to the lighting box.* GUY, *on his own, walks about the stage getting the feel of his costume and feeling slightly sick with nerves. He clears his throat and swings his arms.*
HANNAH *enters with the jacket of his costume.*)

HANNAH: (*Handing it to* GUY) Here. That should be better.

GUY: Thank you.

(GUY *puts on the jacket. There is an awkward formality between them*.)

HANNAH: Let me know if it's still uncomfortable . . .

GUY: No, no. This is perfect.

DAFYDD: (*Emerging briefly in the doorway of the lighting box*) Try circuit 12 plugged into 22. 22, Raymond, 22. My . . . what the hell is it, it's my auxiliary 96. Look, Raymond, next time you re-number the bloody patch field you might tell everybody else about it, will you . . . ? (*He goes inside again*.)

HANNAH: Guy . . . ?

GUY: Yes?

HANNAH: Why haven't you phoned?

GUY: Oh, Hannah . . .

HANNAH: (*Moving to him*) What is it? What have I done? (*They stand together, instinctively clear of the lights and thus out of* DAFYDD's *view*.)

GUY: Look, I've been . . . I've had all this on my mind, haven't I? The play . . .

HANNAH: Is that more important than us?

GUY: No, it's . . . We've been together every evening, for God's sake.

HANNAH: If you call that being together . . .

GUY: Well, it's been very difficult, Hannah. I've only had just over a week to learn the thing . . . (*A brilliant light strikes them both as* RAYMOND *locates another circuit. Instinctively, they both move away*.)

DAFYDD: (*Emerging*) That's fine. Keep that one, don't lose it. Now 27 and 28 should be paired . . . Let's have a look at those. (*Muttering*) Within the next 25 minutes if possible . . . (*He goes in*.)

GUY: Look, there's no point in discussing this now. We can't decide anything in the middle of a –

HANNAH: (*Loudly*) Well, when can we? (*Two more lights illuminate them suddenly.* HANNAH *and* GUY *look towards* DAFYDD.)

DAFYDD: (*Emerging*) Sorry, my loves, I'll be with you in a

minute. Try not to get impatient . . . (*He goes.*)
(HANNAH *and* GUY *move out of the lights again.*)

GUY: All right. If you want to talk about it, we will . . . OK.
I think it's all got to stop. All right? I think it's been
tremendous fun and I think you're wonderful, but it simply
has to stop.

HANNAH: (*Stunned*) What are you talking about? Stop?

DAFYDD: (*Emerging*) Perches one and two. Again, they should
be paired . . . (*He goes.*)

HANNAH: Why? Why?

GUY: Well. For one thing, Dafydd . . .

HANNAH: Dafydd?

GUY: Yes.

HANNAH: Who the hell cares about Dafydd?
(*More lights come up on them again.*)

DAFYDD: (*Emerging again*) I don't like the look of those two.
(HANNAH *and* GUY *move again.*)
Lose them. Give me the other side. Perches 7 and 8, I
think. (*He goes.*)

HANNAH: What's Dafydd got to do with anything?

GUY: Hannah, Dafydd has everything to do with everything. He
is your husband and he's my friend. And if I felt that I was
responsible for your leaving him . . .

HANNAH: I'm leaving him anyway, whether you stay or not, so
that has nothing to do with it . . .
(*A light, this time illuminating them brilliantly from the knees
downwards.* GUY *and* HANNAH *both jump instinctively.*)

GUY: (*Irritably*) Get away . . .

DAFYDD: (*Emerging*) Well, those are no earthly use at all,
Raymond. They're lighting his socks. He'd have to be a
midget. What do you think we're doing, *Snow White*?
FOH 4 then. Let's try that . . . (*He goes.*)

HANNAH: No, I know exactly what you're doing. You're using
Dafydd as an excuse to ditch me, that's all . . .

GUY: That just isn't true . . .
(*More lights come, replacing the others.* GUY *and* HANNAH *are
clear of them.*)

HANNAH: Don't try and pretend to me that you'd consider

85

Dafydd for one single moment . . .

DAFYDD: (*Calling*) I say, you two . . .

HANNAH: . . . if it didn't suit you. It didn't worry you two weeks ago . . .

DAFYDD: (*Calling*) I say, you two –

GUY: I think he wants us . . .

HANNAH: (*Angrily*) Yes?

DAFYDD: (*Coming onstage*) Sorry. Were you running lines? Look, just to save time, would you mind standing for me? I just want to check this focus.

(*He moves* GUY *and* HANNAH *into the lights.*)

Just move into that one, that's right . . . Bit further forward, Hannah. Thank you. Just hold it there.

(DAFYDD *moves away into the auditorium to check the effect.*)

HANNAH: (*As he goes, muttering*) Feeblest excuse I have ever heard in my life . . .

DAFYDD: Hannah, dear, be Annie Anderson for a minute, would you? She's a little taller than you – can you just go up on your toes?

(HANNAH *goes up on tiptoe.*)

Bit more. Thank you.

HANNAH: (*Awkwardly*) I would have preferred it if you'd been honest and said another woman . . .

DAFYDD: Guy, my love . . .

HANNAH: Which, of course, it is.

DAFYDD: Guy, could you go down to Tony Mofitt's size? Would you mind. . . ?

(GUY *crouches low.*)

GUY: About here?

DAFYDD: Fine. Just hold it. (*He considers for a second.*) No, that's not going to work, Raymond. Show me something else . . .

(*During the next, a number of lamps flash on and off the contorted pair, as Raymond offers* DAFYDD, *who is pacing the auditorium, alternative light sources.* DAFYDD *rejects each in turn.*)

HANNAH: (*On the verge of tears again, softly*) I was prepared to give up everything for you, you know . . .

(*A lamp comes on.*)

GUY: (*Softly*) I know, I know . . .

DAFYDD: (*Calling*) No.

HANNAH: (*Softly*) My home, my marriage, even my
children . . .
(*The light goes off and another comes on.*)

GUY: (*Softly*) I don't think you were, Hannah, not if it came
to it . . .

DAFYDD: (*Calling*) No . . .

HANNAH: (*Softly*) I meant every single thing I said to you . . .
(*The light goes off and another goes on.*)

GUY: (*Softly*) I meant everything I said, too . . .

DAFYDD: (*Calling*) No. Not in a million years . . .

HANNAH: (*Softly*) You were playing around with Fay and – God
knows who else. You used me, Guy . . .
(*The light goes off and another goes on.*)

GUY: (*Louder*) That is a lie –

DAFYDD: (*Calling*) Yes! That's it . . . What number's that?
(DAFYDD *rejoins them onstage to check his plan.*
HANNAH *lets out an involuntary moan of misery.*)
(*Looking up at them*) Oh sorry, relax, loves. Sorry. Thanks
for your help. (*He resumes his task.*)
(*A sob from* HANNAH *as they relax their positions. During this*
MR AMES *returns, now in all but full costume.*)

GUY: Hannah . . .

DAFYDD: What's the matter with her?

GUY: Er . . .

DAFYDD: (*Peering at her*) You daft halfpenny, you been staring
into lights again, haven't you? How many times do I have
to tell you? Shut your eyes, girl . . .
(DAFYDD *cuffs her affectionately. He moves away towards*
the lighting box.)

GUY: (*Imploring*) Hannah . . .

HANNAH: (*Deeply miserable*) Oh, Guy . . .

DAFYDD: Now, let me see with that added to it, the state of cue
54 C . . . (*He goes back into the lighting box.*)

HANNAH: I do love you so much, Guy . . .

GUY: I love you, Hannah . . .

87

(*Music starts under. As it does a rather romantic light setting comes up. Presumably Cue 54 C.*)

HANNAH: (*Sings, as Polly*)
O what Pain it is to part!
Can I leave thee, can I leave thee?
O what Pain it is to part!
Can thy Polly ever leave thee?
But lest Death my love should thwart,
And bring thee to the fatal Cart,
Thus I tear thee from my bleeding Heart!
Fly hence, and let me leave thee.

GUY: (*Sings with her, as Macheath*)
But lest death my love should thwart (*etc.*)
(*As the song is ending,* HANNAH *runs from the stage.* GUY *is left standing miserably. The last notes cut off as the lights resume a more natural state.*)

DAFYDD: (*Re-emerges, calling back behind him*) Save that now, Raymond. Save it and replug for the top of the show. God, I think we're there . . .
(DAFYDD *comes down on to the stage.*)
Sorry, Guy. You've been wonderfully patient. Thank you.

GUY: Dafydd . . .

DAFYDD: Yes, my love . . .

GUY: I feel I do have to talk to you about something . . .

DAFYDD: Oh, yes? (*Calling*) Give me the workers, would you, Raymond? And will someone on stage management bring me the A ladders . . . ? Yes. Sorry, Guy. What's the problem?

GUY: Well – it's a ridiculous time to say it but . . .
(*The lights switch to working lights.*)

DAFYDD: (*Yelling*) Thank you. (*Staring up at the spot bar*) I'm going to take this frost out of here, Raymond. I hate it. Passionately. I can't live with a frost up here, I'm sorry . . .
(*Aware that* GUY *is still with him, drawing him aside, quietly*) Guy. Just let me say this. You're going to be sensational, boy. No doubt of it. Just do what you've been doing in rehearsal. The audience are going to lift your game, anyway. You're home and dry . . .

(*During the last, a couple of the stage management now in costume have brought* DAFYDD *the ladders, which they set up for him.*)

GUY: Dafydd, it's not the show I'm talking about . . .

DAFYDD: (*Indicating the ladders*) Would you steady this, I just want to alter something. Ta.

(DAFYDD *shins up the ladders.* GUY *steadies them reluctantly.*)

(*From the top of the ladders*) Now's your chance to get your own back. Tip me off if you want to.

GUY: (*Wearily*) I don't want to do that, Dafydd.

DAFYDD: Ah well, all I can say is, it's a good job it's you down there. There's a whole committee of them back there would do it with pleasure.

(JARVIS *comes on from backstage with part of his costume on.*)

JARVIS: Hey! Is this right?

DAFYDD: (*Barely glancing*) Great, Jarvis. Knockout.

JARVIS: These aren't the right trousers, of course . . . (*He indicates his everyday trousers.*)

DAFYDD: No, no, obviously. It's burnt out, this. (*He examines the frost he has recently removed from the lamp.*)

JARVIS: Nor do they appear to have sent me any boots. The girl's having a look . . .

DAFYDD: Oh, dear . . .

JARVIS: I asked specifically for boots. I wanted some boots. The man's a gaoler, he'd have boots. He'd never have shoes, not in a gaol . . .

DAFYDD: Don't worry, Jarvis, we'll find you some boots, don't worry . . .

JARVIS: Well, I'm not playing him in shoes, that's all. I need to find some boots . . .

(JARVIS *goes off.* DAFYDD *has come down the ladders.*)

DAFYDD: It would help if he found his bloody lines for a kick off. (*Yelling*) Finished with the ladders! (*Showing* GUY *the frame*) Warped. Look at that, eh?

(*He starts to move back towards the lighting box. As* DAFYDD *does so,* IAN, *dressed in his street clothes, strolls in. He carries the evening paper.*)

(*As he goes, to* IAN) What time's this, then? What time's this?

89

IAN: (*Rather aggressively*) Not on till Act Two, am I?

DAFYDD: Fair enough. Fair enough.

IAN: (*To* GUY) Seen the paper, then?

GUY: No. I've not really had time.

IAN: All over the front page. I shouldn't think it'd be much of a surprise to you . . . There you are. Closure Shock. (*To* DAFYDD) BLM's closing . . .

DAFYDD: What's that?

IAN: (*Holding up the paper*) BLM. Closing down . . .
(REBECCA *has entered and stands listening.*)

DAFYDD: Closing down?

IAN: That's what it says . . . 500 jobs gone.

DAFYDD: Oh dear, oh dear . . .

IAN: They're relocating 130 . . .

GUY: One hundred and twenty-eight actually.

IAN: Oh, you did know then?

GUY: Oh, yes.

IAN: I bet you bloody did. Don't miss a trick, do you?

REBECCA: How long have you known this?

GUY: Since I found the note on my desk this morning. Along with most of us. (*Looking at them*) It's true.

IAN: (*Moving away*) I believe you, sunshine . . .

GUY: It's true . . .

IAN: Sure, sure, sure . . . (*He goes.*)

GUY: (*Angrily, after him*) If it makes you feel any better, I don't happen to have been included in the hundred and twenty-eight . . .

REBECCA: I'm hardly surprised . . . (*To* DAFYDD, *indicating her costume*) Do you think this is all right, Dafydd? Since I'm bound to be standing behind some huge tree or something it probably doesn't matter, anyway.

DAFYDD: That's super, Beccy, super . . .

REBECCA: You actually like it?

DAFYDD: It's just right.

REBECCA: (*Moving off*) Oh, well. It's your production, darling. If you're expecting laughs, you won't be disappointed, will you? (*To someone offstage as she goes*) I told you he would. He likes it . . .

(REBECCA *goes off.*)

DAFYDD: (*Yelling*) Come on. Let's get underway. How are you doing, Raymond? Dare I ask? (*He walks into the A ladders.*) I have requested these ladders be moved. Why haven't they? Bridget, somebody. Please.

(DAFYDD *has moved back to* GUY *who sits very miserable in one corner of the stage.* BRIDGET *enters briskly.* DAFYDD *goes to perch on a table to chat to* GUY.)

Guy, I'm desperately sorry to . . .

(BRIDGET *whisks the table from under* DAFYDD. DAFYDD *sits wearily beside* GUY.)

I'm desperately sorry to hear all this, Guy. I really am. Is that what you wanted to tell me, just now? God, I'm sorry. It's just like I said, isn't it? Here we are, playing around with pretty lights and costumes held together with safety pins. Out there it's all happening. (*More positively*) You'll be OK. I know you will. Don't despair, old friend. (*He clasps* GUY *affectionately round the shoulders.*) Excuse me, I'm going to have to light a few fireworks back there . . .

(DAFYDD *goes off. The stage managers have returned and are moving the ladders off.* FAY *comes on with* GUY's *wig and a small mirror.*)

FAY: (*Handing these to* GUY, *coolly*) Here.

GUY: Oh, thank you so much . . .

FAY: She's done what she can with it . . .

GUY: (*Busying himself, examining the wig*) This is fine. Absolutely fine.

FAY: You must be feeling pretty pleased with yourself.

GUY: How do you mean?

FAY: You seem to have succeeded in making fools of most people, haven't you?

GUY: I don't think I have . . . I didn't intend to.

FAY: Calculating little bastard, aren't you? Well, you certainly fooled me. Congratulations. That doesn't often happen. You didn't really convince Ian, I'm afraid. He said you were a shit from the start . . .

GUY: (*Hurt*) Thanks.

(*A silence. The cast begins to assemble onstage. First*
REBECCA. *Then* JARVIS *and then* HANNAH. *All ignore* GUY.
JARVIS *has found some boots from somewhere. He busies
himself putting these on.* REBECCA *hums tunelessly.* BRIDGET
comes in to wait. She is followed by MR AMES.)

BRIDGET: He's coming in a second. He's talking to Ian.
(REBECCA *looks at* FAY. *The silence continues.* TED *and* ENID
enter. They alone seem blissfully unaware of the atmosphere.)

ENID: (*As she comes on, loudly*) Oh yes, they're all . . . Oh. (*Aware
of the silence, in an undertone to* TED) They're all out here . . .
(*Pause.*)
(*Whispering*) I think we're waiting for Dafydd.

TED: (*Whispering*) Yes.

ENID: (*Indicating* TED's *neckware*) Is your bit all right? Do you
want me to tie it again?

TED: No, it's perfect now. Perfect. (*Pause.*) These shoes are a
bit tight.

ENID: Oh, dear.

TED: I was supposed to have some boots but somebody's
pinched them . . .

ENID: Oh, dear.
(LINDA *comes on.*)
Oh, that's better, Linda. That's much better. (*To* TED)
She's taken the ribbon off it. It's better.

TED: Much better . . .
(DAFYDD *enters, somewhat subdued.*)

DAFYDD: Sorry, everyone, but . . . (*He trails away,
his mind obviously elsewhere.*) Right. Sorry. Here we go
then. This is a technical run mostly for stage management
and lighting and so on. But, none the less, do please feel
free to stop if there's anything at all . . . that . . . er . . .
is worrying you. At all. So. Yes. Right. Off we go. Good
luck.
(*Everyone begins to disperse in various directions.* GUY *is one of
the last to leave, having first put on his wig.*)

BRIDGET: (*Yelling as she goes*) Act One beginners stand by
please . . .
(DAFYDD *and* GUY *are alone onstage.*)

DAFYDD: (*Approaching* GUY, *in an undertone*) Ian's just told me, you bastard. About you and Hannah. I just want you to know, I think you are a total and utter bastard. And my one prayer is that one of these days you'll get what's coming to you. OK? That's all I have to say to you.

(DAFYDD *moves off towards the lighting box.* GUY *stands.*)

(*Turning as he goes*) Having said that, all the very best of luck for the show and I hope it goes really well for you. Good luck. (*As he goes*) Come on, Raymond. Let's have the opening state, please . . . Come on. Lights and music.

(GUY *is left onstage. The lights close down to him alone. Prison cell lighting comes up as music starts under.* GUY *is joined as he speaks by* HANNAH *as Polly and* LINDA *as Lucy. We are gradually into the first performance of the production, near the end of Act Three (Scene XV).*)

GUY: (*As Macheath, speaking*) My dear Lucy – My dear Polly – Whatsoever hath past between us is now at an end. – If you are fond of marrying again, the best Advice I can give you, is to ship yourselves off to the West Indies, where you'll have a fair chance of getting a Husband a-piece; or by good Luck, two or three, as you like best.

HANNAH: (*As Polly, speaking*) How can I support this Sight!

LINDA: (*As Lucy, speaking*) There is nothing moves one so much as a great Man in Distress.

(*Singing*) Would I might be hang'd!

HANNAH: (*Singing*) And I would so too!

LINDA: To be hang'd with you.

HANNAH: My Dear, with you.

GUY: (*Singing*) O Leave me to Thought! I fear! I doubt!

I tremble! I droop – See, my Courage is out.

HANNAH: No token of Love?

GUY: See, my Courage is out.

LINDA: No token of Love?

HANNAH: Adieu.

LINDA: Farewell.

GUY: But hark! I hear the Toll of the Bell . . . (*etc.*)

(*During the song the action has moved to Tyburn. A scaffold has been erected. Essentially this is the platform that was centre stage at the start of the play with the addition of a gallows arm. A hooded* HANGMAN *stands waiting there as the rest of the opera is played out.*)

JARVIS: (*Entering as Gaoler*) Four Women more, Captain, with a Child a-piece! See here they come.

(*He gestures.* REBECCA, BRIDGET, FAY *and* ENID *enter with prop babies, making baby-crying noises as they come.*)

GUY: (*As Macheath*) What – four Wives more! – This is too much. – Here – tell the Sherriff's Officers I am ready.

(*A long drumroll. The women hurl aside their babies and with a hiss of anticipation join the rest of the company around the scaffold platform.* GUY, *flanked by two guards* (CRISPIN *and a stage manager*) *approaches. He steps up. The* HANGMAN *prepares to place the noose around his neck. The sound of the crowd and the drumroll increase in volume.* GUY *takes a last look around; at the* HANGMAN, *at the noose and, finally, at the company that has now assembled. A faint look of apprehension passes over his face as he notes their eager faces. Suddenly* TED, *as the Player, appears, apart from the crowd.*)

TED: (*As Player, with a cry*) Wait!

(*Total silence. All on stage, with the exception of* GUY, *freeze totally.* GUY *looks slowly around him.*)

(TED *and* MR AMES, *after a moment, also unfreeze.*)

TED: (*To* MR AMES) Honest Friend, I hope you don't intend that Macheath shall be really executed.

MR AMES: (*As Beggar, at the piano*) Most certainly, Sir – To make the Piece perfect, I was for doing strict poetical Justice. – Macheath is to be hang'd; and for the other Personages of the Drama, the Audience must have suppos'd they were all either hang'd or transported.

TED: Why then, Friend, this is down-right deep Tragedy. The Catastrophe is manifestly wrong, for an Opera must end happily. All this we must do to comply with the Taste of the Town.

MR AMES: Your Objection, Sir, is very just; and is easily remov'd. For you must allow, that in this kind of Drama, 'tis no matter how absurdly things are brought about – So

(with a snap of his fingers and the gesture of a magician. . .)
(IAN rushes on in his Matt of the Mint costume, brandishing an official document.)

IAN: A reprieve! A reprieve for Macheath!

ALL: *(In an awed murmur)* A reprieve?

(IAN gives the document to the HANGMAN who reads it.)

HANGMAN: A reprieve!

ALL: A Reprieve for Macheath!

(A great deal of cheering. The gallows arm is removed. All push forward to congratulate the prisoner. The HANGMAN, removing his hood, reveals he is DAFYDD. He embraces GUY. A serving wench brings ale for them both.)

GUY: *(As Macheath, holding up his hands for silence)* So, it seems, I am not left to my Choice, but must have a Wife at last – Look ye, my Dears, we will have no Controversie now. Let us give this Day to Mirth, and I am sure she who thinks herself my Wife will testifie her Joy by a Dance.

ALL: Come, a Dance – a Dance.

GUY: *(Sings)* Thus I stand like a Turk, with his Doxies around;
From all Sides their Glances his Passion confound;
For, black, brown and fair, his Inconstancy burns,
And the different Beauties subdue him by turns:
Each calls forth her Charms, to provoke his Desires:
Though willing to all; with but one he retires.
But think of this Maxim, and Put off your Sorrow,
The Wretch of To-day, may be happy To-morrow.

CHORUS: But think of this maxim *(etc.)*

(This time, as with The Beggar's Opera *itself, the performance ends happily and triumphantly (if a trifle cynically). The actors take their curtain calls. As the curtain falls for the last time they embrace each other, most especially their hero of the night, GUY himself. Relieved and exalted, they return to their dressing rooms.)*